Practice 1.1

Name ______________________________ Date ______________

Uses of Numbers

Tell how each number is used. Write *position, count, measure,* or *label* for each.

1. 

____

2. 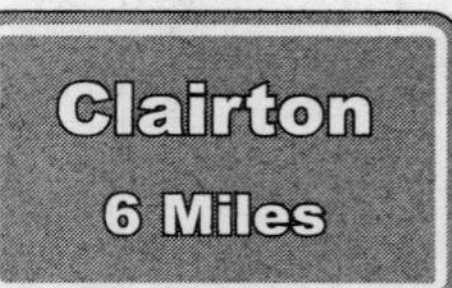

____

3. 

____

4. 21 miles ______________

5. first at bat ______________

6. Flight 407 ______________

7. 9 footballs ______________

8. 4 Elm Street ______________

9. 5 gallons ______________

Complete.

10. second, third, __________, fifth

11. __________, third, fourth

12. fifth, __________, seventh, eighth

13. sixth, __________, eighth, __________

14. Which number is used as a measure?

A third inning **C** 36 books

B Apartment 4 **D** 50 yards

15. Use the number 5 in three different ways.

____

____

____

____

____

Use with text pages 4–5.

Name ____________________ Date ____________

Practice 1.2

Place Value: Ones, Tens, and Hundreds

Write each number in standard form.

1. 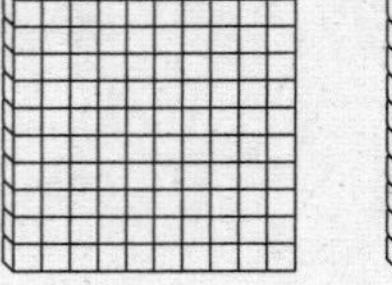 ______

2. 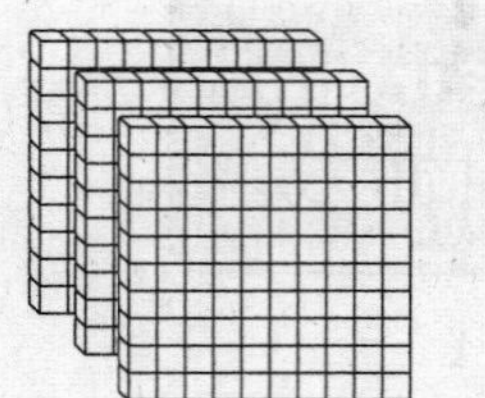 ______

3. 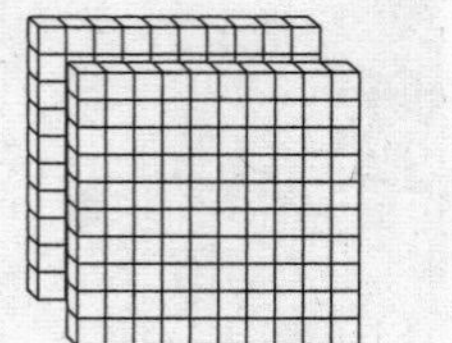 ______

4. 700 + 50 + 4 ______

5. 300 + 9 ______

6. 100 + 10 + 1 ______

7. eight hundred thirteen ____________________

8. four hundred eighty ____________________

Write the place of the underlined digit. Then write its value.

9. 582 ____________________

10. 703 ____________________

11. 266 ____________________

12. 847 ____________________

13. Which number has a 4 in the hundreds place?

A 354 **C** 534

B 453 **D** 543

14. Is 600 + 2 the expanded form of 632? Explain how you know.

____

____

____

Use with text pages 6–7.

Name ______________________ Date ____________

Practice 1.3

How Big Is One Thousand?

Tell if each is *greater than, less than,* or *equal to* 1,000.

1. 8 boxes of 1000 counters

____

2. 1 bag of 1,000 marbles

____

3. 5 trays of 100 cookies

____

4. 9 rolls of 100 stamps

____

5. 10 packs of 10 markers

____

6. 8 pages of 100 pictures

____

7. 10 boxes of 1,000 paint brushes

____

8. 10 boxes of 100 books

____

9. 2 boxes of 1,000 crayons

____

10. 2 bags of 100 marbles

____

Test Prep

11. Which is NOT equal to 1,000 peanuts?

A 10 bags of 100 peanuts

B 100 bags of 10 peanuts

C 10 bags of 10 peanuts

D 1 bag of 1,000 peanuts

____

12. Are 10 cans in each of 10 boxes equal to 1,000? Explain how you know.

____

____

____

____

Name ______________________ Date ____________

Practice 1.4

Place Value Through Thousands

Write each number in two other ways. Use standard form, expanded form, and word form.

1. 2,000 + 300 + 10 + 4

2. 8,000 + 400 + 6

3. three thousand, six hundred 2

4. 9 thousand, twenty

5. eight thousand, two

6. four thousand, fifteen

Write the place of the underlined digit. Then write its value.

7. 6,1<u>3</u>5

8. <u>7</u>,042

9. 2,<u>1</u>58

10. <u>5</u>,989

Test Prep

11. Which number shows six thousand, sixty-six?

A 6,006

B 6,066

C 6,660

D 6,666

Use with text pages 10–12.

Name ______________________ Date ______________

Practice 1.5

Problem-Solving Strategy: Find a Number Pattern

Use a number pattern to solve each problem.

Show your work.

1. Sandy played in 4 soccer games in May, 7 soccer games in June, 10 soccer games in July, and 13 soccer games in August. If the pattern continues, in how many soccer games is Sandy likely to play in September?

____

2. Four lockers in the gym are numbered 15, 17, 19, and 21. If the pattern continues, what is the number of the next locker likely to be?

____

3. Horus sold 4 tickets for the soccer tournament on Monday, 5 tickets on Tuesday, 7 tickets on Wednesday, and 10 tickets on Thursday. If the pattern continues, how many tickets is Horus likely to sell on Saturday?

____

4. What is the next number in the pattern below likely to be?

   14, 24, 34, 44, ______

5. What are the next two numbers in the pattern below likely to be?

   235, 230, 225, 220, ______, ______

Use with text pages 14–16.

Name ______________________ Date ____________

Place Value Through Ten Thousands

Write each number in standard form.

1. 40,000 + 300 + 70 + 6

2. 10,000 + 7,000 + 800 + 2

3. 50,000 + 1,000 + 4

4. 20,000 + 9,000 + 800 + 40

5. three thousand, six hundred seven

6. eighteen thousand, five hundred nineteen

7. forty thousand, seventy-nine

8. ten thousand, two

Write the place of the underlined digit. Then write its value.

9. 29,643

10. 32,015

11. 7,682

12. 82,444

13. Which is another way to write 60,000 + 3,000 + 700 + 5?

A 6,375 **C** 63,705

B 63,075 **D** 63,750

14. Which digit has the greatest value in the number 14,789? Explain how you found your answer.

Use with text pages 18–19.

Name ______________________ Date ____________

Practice 1.7

Place Value Through Hundred Thousands

Write each number in standard form.

1. 700,000 + 20,000 + 4,000 + 500 + 60 + 2

____

2. 500,000 + 10,000 + 600 + 40 + 3

____

3. four hundred thirty-six thousand, seven hundred ninety-four

____

4. five hundred nineteen thousand, twenty-three

____

Write the place of the underlined digit. Then write its value.

5. 7<u>2</u>9,058

____

____

6. <u>6</u>48,549

____

____

7. 321,<u>5</u>67

____

____

8. 83<u>9</u>,061

____

____

Test Prep

9. Which number has the same digit in the hundred thousands place, the thousands place, and the hundreds place?

A 449,462 C 494,642

B 494,462 D 944,462

10. What digit is in the ten thousands place in the number six hundred three thousand, twenty-one? Explain how you found your answer.

____

____

____

Name Austin Date

Practice 2.1

Compare Numbers

Compare. Write >, <, or = for each ○.

1. 43 ○ 41
2. 52 ○ 72
3. 90 ○ 87
4. 36 ○ 36
5. 154 ○ 134
6. 175 ○ 125
7. 138 ○ 192
8. 217 ○ 184
9. 129 ○ 93
10. 645 ○ 645
11. 705 ○ 792
12. 586 ○ 986
13. 1,792 ○ 1,792
14. 2,046 ○ 2,135
15. 4,635 ○ 3,287
16. 9,068 ○ 9,014

Write = or ≠ for each ○.

17. 15 + 3 ○ 17
18. 13 + 4 ○ 17
19. 30 + 8 ○ 39
20. 60 + 5 ○ 62
21. 20 + 8 ○ 28
22. 100 + 30 ○ 130
23. 200 + 9 ○ 290
24. 300 + 90 ○ 39
25. 100 + 20 ○ 1,200

Test Prep

26. Use the table below to answer the question. Which river has a length that is less than the Ucayali River?

World Rivers	
Name	**Length (in miles)**
Angara	1,151
Dniester	877
Magdalena	956
Senegal	1,020
Ucayali	910

A Angara
B Dniester
C Magdalena
D Senegal

27. Nancy found the heights of some mountains in North Carolina. She found that Mount Mitchell is 6,684 feet tall and Mount Craig is 6,647 feet tall. Which mountain is taller? Explain how you got your answer.

MOV1t Mitchell is hier then MOV1t crag becus 6,684 is grater then 6,647

Name ________________________ Date ______________

Practice 2.2

Order Numbers

Write the numbers in order from least to greatest.

1. 29 23 18
______

2. 34 41 30
______

3. 82 57 61
______

4. 126 105 94
______

5. 273 223 409
______

6. 559 317 563
______

7. 1,013 986 1,103
______

8. 2,894 3,157 3,175
______

9. 5,583 2,397 6,490
______

Write the numbers in order from greatest to least.

10. 774 86 1,056
______

11. 1,608 6,803 680
______

12. 9,537 9,539 9,812
______

13. Judy made a table to show the length of three rivers. What is the correct order of the rivers from greatest to least length?

World Rivers

Name	Length (in miles)
Tigris	1,180
Oka	932
Songhua	1,150

A Tigris, Oka, Songhua

B Oka, Songhua, Tigris

C Songhua, Tigris, Oka

D Tigris, Songhua, Oka

14. David found the heights of three volcanoes. He found that the Manam volcano is 5,928 feet tall, the Karkar volcano is 6,033 feet tall, and the Bandai volcano is 5,968 feet tall. What is the correct order of the volcanoes from least to greatest height? Explain how you got your answer.

______
______
______
______

Use with text pages 30–31.

Name ______________________________ Date ______________

Practice 2.3

Round Two-Digit and Three-Digit Numbers

For each number, write the 2 tens the number is between. Then round to the nearest ten.

1. 28 ________ **2.** 41 ________ **3.** 84 ________ **4.** 79 ________

5. 682 ________ **6.** 376 ________ **7.** 146 ________ **8.** 812 ________

For each number, write the 2 hundreds the number is between. Then round to the nearest hundred.

9. 505 ________ **10.** 693 ________ **11.** 872 ________ **12.** 724 ________

Round to the place of the underlined digit.

13. $\underline{1}6$ ________ **14.** $\underline{2}81$ ________ **15.** $1\underline{1}3$ ________ **16.** $7\underline{3}5$ ________

17. $\underline{5}36$ ________ **18.** $4\underline{5}2$ ________ **19.** $\underline{6}57$ ________ **20.** $\underline{8}95$ ________

Test Prep

21. Four friends picked apples on a farm. Cora picked 267 apples. Ed picked 212 apples. Tim picked 238 apples. Yuki picked 249 apples. Rounded to the nearest hundred, who picked about 300 apples?

A Cora **C** Tim

B Ed **D** Yuki

Use with text pages 32–34.

Name ______________________ Date ______________

Practice 2.4

Round Four-Digit Numbers

Round to the place of the underlined digit.

1. 1,<u>6</u>75	**2.** 2,3<u>8</u>1	**3.** <u>1</u>,613	**4.** <u>3</u>,406	**5.** 4,5<u>0</u>9
______	______	______	______	______
6. <u>3</u>,734	**7.** 4<u>8</u>1	**8.** 8,<u>1</u>13	**9.** <u>6</u>02	**10.** 5,<u>4</u>07
______	______	______	______	______
11. 3<u>8</u>6	**12.** 2,2<u>7</u>3	**13.** <u>6</u>,510	**14.** 3,<u>7</u>82	**15.** 8,<u>3</u>08
______	______	______	______	______
16. <u>5</u>,629	**17.** 1,0<u>2</u>5	**18.** <u>9</u>14	**19.** 2<u>9</u>7	**20.** <u>9</u>,403
______	______	______	______	______
21. <u>5</u>32	**22.** 4,<u>8</u>57	**23.** <u>3</u>,225	**24.** 7,9<u>9</u>4	**25.** 8,<u>0</u>66
______	______	______	______	______

Test Prep

26. Pepper Pike's population was about 6,040 in 2000 and about 6,185 in 1990. What was the population of Pepper Pike in 1990, rounded to the nearest hundred?

A 6,100 **C** 6,190

B 6,110 **D** 6,200

27. Mrs. Davis drove 1,058 miles to visit her aunt in Dayton. How many miles did Mrs. Davis drive, rounded to the nearest ten? Explain how you got your answer.

____

____

Use with text pages 36–37.

Name ______________________ Date __________

Practice 2.5

Problem-Solving Application: Use a Bar Graph

Use Data A high school band performed on four nights. The bar graph on the left shows the number of people who attended each night. The bar graph on the right shows the number of CDs sold each night.

Use the bar graphs to solve each problem.

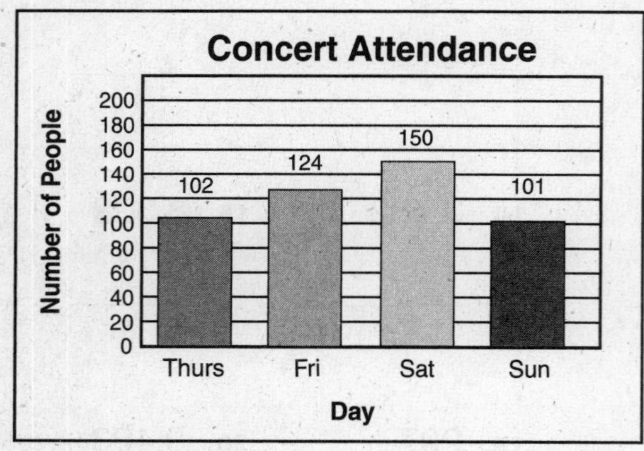

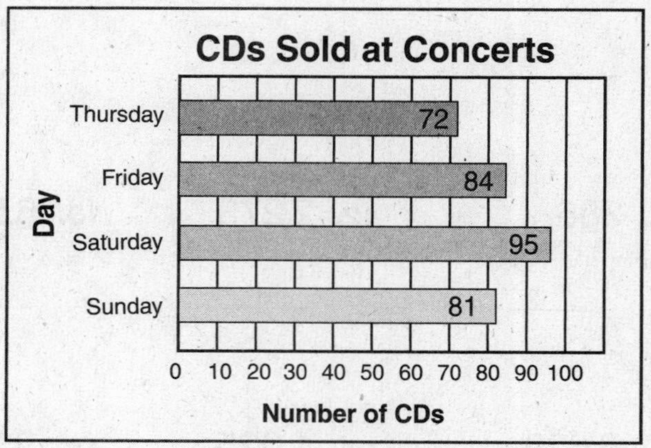

1. Which night did the most people attend the concert? How many people attended that night?

____

2. Which night were the fewest CDs sold at the concerts? How many CDs were sold that night?

____

3. Which two days had about the same number of people attending the concert?

____

4. To the nearest ten, how many CDs were sold on Sunday?

____

Name ______________________ Date ____________

Practice 3.1

Value of Money

Write each amount using a dollar sign and a decimal point.

1. 

____

2. 

____

3. 

____

4. 

____

5. four dollars and thirteen cents

____

6. six dollars and eight cents

____

Test Prep

7. Marco has 2 dollars and 9 dimes. What is the total value of the money Marco has?

   A $2.90 C $2.19

   B $2.09 D $0.29

8. Lori has $4.31 in her piggy bank. How much will she have if she adds 1 dollar, 5 dimes, and 6 pennies? Using a dollar sign and a decimal point, write the total amount of money in Lori's piggy bank.

____

Use with text pages 46–47.

Name ______________________ Date ____________

Practice 3.2

Count Coins and Bills

Write each amount using a dollar sign and a decimal point.

1. 

____

2. 

____

3. 

____

4. 

____

5. 1 five-dollar bill, 2 one-dollar bills, 3 quarters, 2 dimes

____

6. 1 ten-dollar bill, 1 one-dollar bill, 1 half-dollar, 1 quarter, 3 pennies

____

Test Prep

7. Jamie paid for a notebook using these bills and coins.

What is the value of the money Jamie paid?

A \$32.41 **C** \$3.95

B \$30.91 **D** \$3.41

8. Tom has 4 one-dollar bills, 2 dimes and 4 pennies. Using a dollar sign and a decimal point, write the amount of money Tom has.

____

Use with text pages 48–49.

Name ______________________ Date ____________

Practice 3.3

Problem-Solving Application: Make Change

Use the school store items below to solve each problem.

Problems | **Show Your Work**

1. Kendall buys a spiral notebook. She pays with a five-dollar bill. How much change should she receive?

____

2. Pablo buys a three-ring binder. He pays with a ten-dollar bill. How much change should he receive? List the coins and bills he might receive as change.

____

____

3. Rachel buys a pencil. She pays with $1.00. Then she uses her change to buy a sticker. How much money does Rachel have left?

____

Use with text pages 50–51.

Name ______________________ Date ____________

Practice 3.4

Compare Money Amounts

Compare. Write >, <, or = for each ○.

1.   ○   

2.  ○ 

3.  ○   

4.  ○   

Test Prep

5. Jess has 2 five-dollar bills, 1 one-dollar bill, 2 quarters, and 1 nickel. Which of these amounts is greater than the total amount of money that Jess has?

A $11.50 **C** $10.56

B $11.60 **D** $6.80

6. Mandy has 1 half-dollar, 1 quarter, 1 dime, and 2 nickels. What is another set of coins with the same value as Mandy's coins? List the coins.

____

____

____

Use with text pages 52–54.

Name ______________________ Date ____________

Round Money

Round to the nearest dollar.

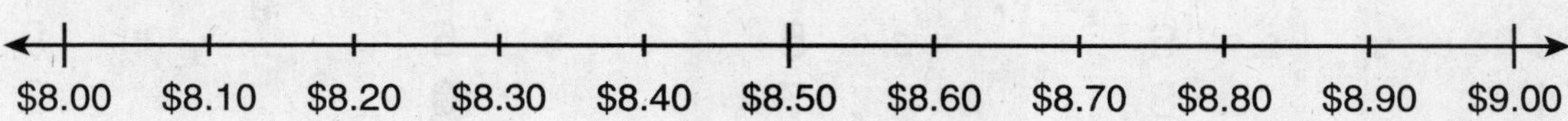

1. $8.75 ______ **2.** $8.65 ______ **3.** $8.45 ______ **4.** $8.15 ______

Round to the nearest ten dollars.

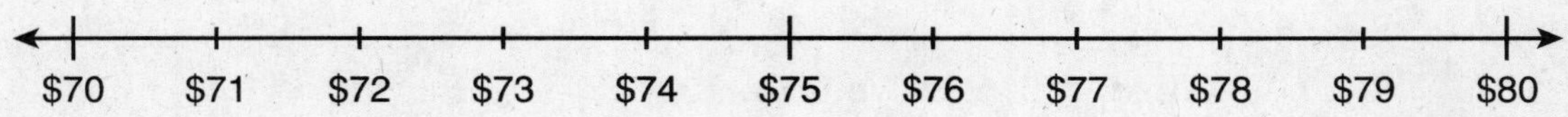

5. $71.86 ______ **6.** $74.93 ______ **7.** $79.02 ______ **8.** $77.38 ______

9. $78.05 ______ **10.** $73.68 ______ **11.** $70.36 ______ **12.** $75.82 ______

Round each amount to the place of the underlined digit.

13. $<u>1</u>.68 ______ **14.** $<u>2</u>8.15 ______ **15.** $1<u>1</u>.87 ______ **16.** $<u>4</u>.09 ______

17. $<u>5</u>3.64 ______ **18.** $4<u>3</u>.76 ______ **19.** $<u>3</u>0.36 ______ **20.** $<u>8</u>9.52 ______

Test Prep

21. Trent has $26.75. Nelly has $21.25. Ricardo has $23.83. Frank has $24.90. Which of the four friends has about $30.00?

A Frank **C** Nelly

B Ricardo **D** Trent

22. Caitlin collected $43.90 for her school's food drive. What is the amount Caitlin collected rounded to the nearest ten dollars?

____

Use with text pages 56–58.

Name ______________________ Date ____________

Practice 4.1

Addition Properties

Find each sum.

1. 3 + 4 + 7 (vertical: 3, 4, +7) ____

2. 6 + 8 + 2 (vertical: 6, 8, +2) ____

3. 5 + 7 + 5 (vertical: 5, 7, +5) ____

4. 6 + 0 + 9 (vertical: 6, 0, +9) ____

5. 9 + 3 + 4 (vertical: 9, 3, +4) ____

6. 3 + 6 = ____
6 + 3 = ____

7. 2 + 5 = ____
5 + 2 = ____

8. 4 + 9 = ____
9 + 4 = ____

9. 8 + 0 = ____

10. 0 + 1 = ____

11. 0 + 7 = ____

12. 4 + (7 + 2) = ____

13. (6 + 4) + 7 = ____

14. 8 + (1 + 9) = ____

15. 4 + (3 + 8) + 5 = ____

16. 1 + 7 + (6 + 6) = ____

17. (7 + 8) + 5 + 2 = ____

Test Prep

18. Michael found that it rained on 3 days in June. He found that it rained on 9 days in July and 7 days in August. How many days did it rain in June, July, and August altogether?

A 20 **C** 18

B 19 **D** 16

19. Three friends collected baseball cards. They collected 16 cards in all. Josie collected 8 cards. Andy collected 4 cards. How many cards did the third friend collect? Explain how you found your answer.

____

____

Use with text pages 76–77.

Name ______________________ Date __________

Practice 4.2

Estimate Sums

Round each number to the greatest place. Then add.

1. 49 + 71
2. 32 + 54
3. 62 + 84
4. 71 + 48
5. 58 + 89
6. 37 + 46
7. 21 + 34
8. 36 + 79
9. 73 + 65
10. 82 + 46
11. 91 + 25
12. $2.37 + 1.94
13. $3.58 + 2.07
14. 973 + 98
15. 175 + 886
16. $1.27 + $2.99 ______
17. 281 + 834 ______
18. 762 + 519 ______
19. $5.70 + $3.15 ______
20. 607 + 932 ______
21. 985 + 97 ______
22. $3.67 + $8.79 ______
23. 972 + 158 ______

Test Prep

24. Yoshi bought some lunch. He spent $4.65 on a sandwich and $1.09 on a drink. About how much did Yoshi spend in all for lunch?

   A $4.00 C $6.00

   B $5.00 D $7.00

25. The Clark family took a car trip. They drove 872 miles in one week. Then, they drove 114 miles the next day. About how many miles did the family drive in all? Explain how you got your answer.

____

____

____

Use with text pages 78–80.

Name ______________________ Date ____________

Practice 4.3

Regroup Ones

Find each sum. Estimate to check.

1. 27 + 56
2. 76 + 18
3. 165 + 229
4. 438 + 357
5. 567 + 425
6. 64 + 29
7. \$2.37 + 1.24
8. \$3.59 + 2.09
9. 703 + 169
10. 285 + 606
11. 809 + 164
12. 687 + 207
13. 556 + 436
14. \$3.48 + 1.15
15. \$1.29 + 6.38

Algebra • Functions
Complete each table by following the rule.

	Rule: Add 26	
	Input	Output
16.	67	
17.	49	
18.	58	
19.	73	

	Rule: Add 137	
	Input	Output
20.	225	
21.	348	
22.	154	
23.	439	

	Rule: Add \$129	
	Input	Output
24.	\$243	
25.	\$807	
26.	\$362	
27.	\$556	

Test Prep

28. Neal bought a tomato plant for \$3.29. He bought some plant food for \$2.68. What was the total cost of the tomato plant and plant food?

A \$5.87 C \$6.87

B \$5.97 D \$6.97

29. The town of Easton had a fair. On Friday, 279 people attended the fair. On Saturday, 406 people attended the fair. How many people attended the town fair on both days altogether? Explain how you got your answer.

____

____

Use with text pages 82–84.

Name ______________________ Date ____________

Practice 4.4

Regroup Ones and Tens

Add. Check by adding upward.

1. 143 + 225
2. 164 + 223
3. 129 + 157
4. 427 + 255
5. 693 + 124
6. 143 + 282
7. $3.29 + 1.69
8. $1.18 + 2.77
9. 725 + 198
10. 286 + 546
11. 366 + 258
12. 437 + 199
13. 249 + 573
14. $2.64 + 6.58
15. $3.42 + 5.89

Algebra • Functions
Follow the rule to complete each table.

	Rule: Add 67	
	Input	**Output**
16.	25	
17.	16	
18.	19	
19.	23	

	Rule: Add 239	
	Input	**Output**
20.	346	
21.	402	
22.	153	
23.	529	

	Rule: Add $218	
	Input	**Output**
24.	$162	
25.	$345	
26.	$679	
27.	$457	

Test Prep

28. Rita's class collected books for a book sale. The students collected 187 books in the first month. They collected 209 books in the second month. How many books did the students collect in all?

A 22
B 386
C 396
D 397

29. Eric bought bread for $2.39. He bought apples for $2.58. What was the total cost of the bread and apples? Explain how you got your answer.

____

____

Use with text pages 86–88.

Name ______________________ Date ____________

Practice 4.5

Problem-Solving Strategy: Guess and Check

Use guess and check to solve each problem.

Show your work.

1. The Jacksons have pet dogs named Beau and Max. Beau is 2 years older than Max. The sum of their ages is 16 years. How old is Beau? How old is Max?

   ____

   ____

2. Together, Misty and Keith caught 29 fish this summer. Keith caught 5 fewer fish than Misty. How many fish did Misty catch? How many fish did Keith catch?

   ____

   ____

3. The Nature Center has 50 reptiles and birds on exhibit. There are 20 more birds than reptiles. How many reptiles are on exhibit at the Nature Center? How many birds?

   ____

   ____

4. Koalas and sloths are very sleepy animals. Together, a koala and a sloth can sleep 42 hours a day. Suppose a koala sleeps 2 hours more than a sloth. How long does each animal sleep?

   ____

Use with text pages 90–92.

Name ______________________ Date ____________

Practice 4.6

Column Addition

Add. Check by adding in a different order.

1. $$\begin{array}{r} 28 \\ 15 \\ +36 \\ \hline \end{array}$$

2. $$\begin{array}{r} 45 \\ 29 \\ +23 \\ \hline \end{array}$$

3. $$\begin{array}{r} 17 \\ 56 \\ +21 \\ \hline \end{array}$$

4. $$\begin{array}{r} 38 \\ 42 \\ +16 \\ \hline \end{array}$$

5. $$\begin{array}{r} 129 \\ 57 \\ +\ 12 \\ \hline \end{array}$$

6. $$\begin{array}{r} 597 \\ 144 \\ +138 \\ \hline \end{array}$$

7. $$\begin{array}{r} 86 \\ 203 \\ +514 \\ \hline \end{array}$$

8. $$\begin{array}{r} \$1.41 \\ 4.09 \\ +\ 2.75 \\ \hline \end{array}$$

9. $$\begin{array}{r} 24 \\ 112 \\ 763 \\ +\ 98 \\ \hline \end{array}$$

10. $$\begin{array}{r} 247 \\ 103 \\ 395 \\ +231 \\ \hline \end{array}$$

11. 35 + 27 + 14 ____________

12. 124 + 36 + 93 + 45 ____________

13. 476 + 29 + 43 ____________

Algebra • Symbols
Use >,< or = for each ◯.

14. 25 + 0 ◯ 25 − 0

15. 124 + 42 ◯ 124 + 45

16. 27 + 55 ◯ 47 + 17

17. 14 + 57 ◯ 57 + 14

Test Prep

18. The Rios family drove 16 miles to visit a museum. Then, the family drove 28 miles to visit a farm. Finally, the family drove 34 miles to a camp. How many miles did the Rios family drive in all?

A 44 **C** 68

B 62 **D** 78

19. Forty-five students bought a lunch on Monday. Eighteen students bought a lunch on Tuesday. Thirty students bought a lunch on Wednesday. How many lunches were bought over the 3 days? Explain how you got your answer.

____

____

Use with text pages 94–96.

Name ______________________ Date ____________

Practice 4.7

Add Greater Numbers

Find each sum. Estimate to check.

1. 1,498 + 3,264

2. 2,437 + 3,196

3. 1,342 + 2,065 + 3,427

4. 2,053 + 2,146 + 3,287

5. 2,586 + 1,945

6. $36.75 + 12.48

7. 3,679 + 2,638

8. 184 + 405 + 287

9. $23.79 + 15.38

10. 1,267 + 3,948

11. $19.41 + 32.76

12. 4,065 + 1,337 + 3,592

13. 3,876 + 2,696

14. 4,937 + 3,954

15. 2,373 + 2,209 + 3,564

16. $34.29 + 16.65

Test Prep

17. Mount Washington in New Hampshire is 1,427 feet taller than Spruce Knob Mountain in West Virginia. Spruce Knob Mountain is 4,861 feet tall. How many feet tall is Mount Washington?

A 3,436 **C** 7,288

B 6,288 **D** 51,288

18. Tammy's sister earned $24.72 at her job on Friday. She earned $32.96 at her job on Saturday. What is the total amount that Tammy's sister earned on the two days? Explain how you got your answer.

____

____

Use with text pages 98–99.

Name ______________________ Date ____________

Practice 4.8

Choose a Method

Add. Choose mental math, paper and pencil, or calculator. Explain your choice.

1. 40 + 19

2. 37 + 25

3. 49 + 51

4. 320 + 165

5. 638 + 294

6. 87 + 30

7. 302 + 418

8. 750 + 210

9. 1,300 + 2,450

10. 1,756 + 2,384

11. 590 + 110

12. 274 + 569

13. 125 + 275

14. 2,200 + 1,398

15. 1,899 + 4,100

16. 435 + 347 + 205

____

17. $4.95 + $1.75 + $3.25

____

Test Prep

18. Pedro collected 18 rocks. He collected 30 leaves. He collected 25 shells. How many rocks, leaves, and shells did he collect in all?

A 73 C 68

B 72 D 65

19. There were 20 school days in March, 22 school days in April, and 18 school days in May. How many school days were there in the three months?

____

Use with text pages 100–101.

Name ______________________ Date ______________

Practice 4.9

Problem-Solving Decision: Estimate or Exact Answer

Solve. Tell whether you need an exact answer or an estimate.

Show your work.

1. A baby giraffe is 72 inches tall at birth. His mother is 156 inches taller. How tall is the mother giraffe?

____

2. An African elephant weighs about 6,500 pounds more than a white rhinoceros. The rhinoceros weighs 7,037 pounds. About how much does the elephant weigh?

____

3. An anaconda is 24 inches longer than a king cobra. The cobra is 216 inches long. How long is the anaconda?

____

4. Two baby walruses each weigh 139 pounds. The mother walrus weighs 1,820 pounds. Do the two babies together weigh more or less than their mother?

____

5. Every day, a blue whale calf drinks about 528 pints of milk. Is 900 pints of milk enough to feed two blue whale calves for one day? Explain.

____

Use with text page 102.

Name ______________________ Date ____________

Practice 5.1

Subtraction Rules

Subtract. Use subtraction rules when you can.

1. $54 - 0 =$ ____
2. $9 - 9 =$ ____
3. $16 - 0 =$ ____
4. $33 - 33 =$ ____
5. $25 - 15 =$ ____
6. $77 - 77 =$ ____
7. $65 - 65 =$ ____
8. $15 - 10 =$ ____
9. $85 - 0 =$ ____
10. $26 - 2 =$ ____
11. $36 - 0$ ____
12. $74 - 74$ ____
13. $19 - 4$ ____
14. $24 - 0$ ____
15. $17 - 5$ ____
16. $35 - 35$ ____
17. $13 - 0$ ____
18. $25 - 0$ ____
19. $25 - 5$ ____
20. $30 - 0$ ____

Algebra • Properties Find each missing number.

21. $17 - ■ = 0$ ____
22. $■ - 18 = 0$ ____
23. $0 = 66 - ■$ ____
24. $14 - 0 = ■$ ____
25. $■ - 33 = 0$ ____
26. $0 = ■ - 41$ ____
27. $36 - ■ = 0$ ____
28. $22 - 0 = ■$ ____

Test Prep

29. What is the difference when 0 is subtracted from 29?

 A 58 C 29

 B 14 D 0

30. Jeffrey washed 24 grapes. At lunch, he eats 24 grapes. How many grapes are left? Explain how you know.

____

____

Use with text pages 108–109.

Name ______________________ Date ____________

Practice 5.2

Relate Addition and Subtraction

Use counters to find each missing number.

1. $5 + 4 = 9$
   $9 - 4 = \blacksquare$

2. $9 + 7 = 16$
   $16 - 7 = \blacksquare$

3. $3 + 7 = 10$
   $10 - \blacksquare = 7$

4. $8 + \blacksquare = 12$
   $12 - 8 = 4$

5. $9 + 5 = 14$
   $14 - 9 = \blacksquare$

6. $\blacksquare + 7 = 10$
   $10 - 7 = 3$

7. $5 + 6 = 11$
   $11 - 5 = \blacksquare$

8. $8 + 9 = 17$
   $\blacksquare - 8 = 9$

Complete each fact family.

9. $2 + 6 = 8$
   $6 + \blacksquare = 8$
   $8 - 6 = \blacksquare$
   $8 - \blacksquare = 6$

10. $9 + 6 = 15$
    $6 + \blacksquare = 15$
    $15 - 6 = \blacksquare$
    $15 - \blacksquare = 6$

11. $8 + 6 = 14$
    $6 + \blacksquare = 14$
    $14 - 6 = \blacksquare$
    $14 - \blacksquare = 6$

12. $5 + 3 = 8$
    $3 + \blacksquare = 8$
    $8 - 5 = \blacksquare$
    $8 - \blacksquare = 5$

13. $8 + 2 = 10$
    $2 + \blacksquare = 10$
    $10 - \blacksquare = 8$
    $10 - \blacksquare = 2$

14. $5 + 7 = 12$
    $7 + \blacksquare = 12$
    $12 - \blacksquare = 7$
    $\blacksquare - 7 = 5$

15. $12 + 6 = 18$
    $6 + \blacksquare = 18$
    $18 - 6 = \blacksquare$
    $18 - 12 = \blacksquare$

16. $6 + 7 = 13$
    $\blacksquare + 6 = 13$
    $13 - \blacksquare = 7$
    $\blacksquare - 7 = 6$

Test Prep

17. Karen wrote $35 - 12 = 23$. Which addition sentence could she use to check her answer?

    A $23 + 10 = 33$

    B $12 + 10 = 22$

    C $23 + 13 = 36$

    D $23 + 12 = 35$

18. Daniel has 8 blue marbles and 3 green marbles. He says that he has 11 marbles in all. Write two subtraction sentences that could be used to check if Daniel is right.

    ____

    ____

Use with text pages 110–111.

Name ______________________ Date ____________

Practice 5.3

Estimate Differences

Round each number to the greatest place. Then subtract.

1. 84 − 51

2. 92 − 44

3. 32 − 16

4. 517 − 363

5. 836 − 287

6. 334 − 232

7. \$632 − \$221 ______

8. \$402 − \$112 ______

9. 289 − 122 ______

10. \$931 − \$814 ______

11. \$4.92 − \$3.18 ______

12. \$7.75 − \$3.18 ______

13. \$901 − \$576 ______

14. 489 − 123 ______

15. \$9.01 − \$5.76 ______

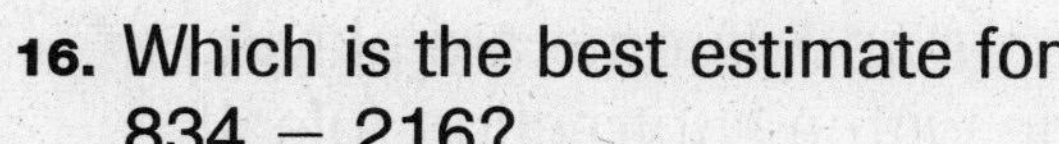

16. Which is the best estimate for 834 − 216?

A 600 **C** 800

B 700 **D** 900

17. Jeffrey collects toy cars. He has 385 toys in his collection. If he sells 141 cars, about how many will he have left? Explain how you found your answer.

____

____

Use with text pages 112–114.

Name ______________________ Date ______________

Practice 5.4

Regroup Tens

Find each difference. Estimate to check.

1. 46 − 17

2. 87 − 38

3. 51 − 25

4. 86 − 17

5. 97 − 79

6. 322 − 15

7. 836 − 429

8. 437 − 218

9. 964 − 447

10. $683 − $256

11. 433 − 115 ______

12. 262 − 134 ______

13. 692 − 267 ______

14. $721 − $707 ______

15. $952 − $436 ______

16. 336 − 219 ______

17. 792 − 424 ______

18. $837 − $306 ______

Algebra • Functions **Complete each table.**

	Rule: Subtract 48.	
	Input	**Output**
19.	62	
20.	78	
21.	85	

	Rule: Subtract $147	
	Input	**Output**
22.	$463	
23.		$288
24.		$376

Test Prep

25. Nancy has $684 in her checking account. If she writes a check for $456 to pay her rent, how much is left in the account?

A $226 C $228

B $232 D $238

26. Marcus and Jerome are playing a game with a subtraction rule. If Marcus says “745,” Jerome says “616.” If Marcus says “181,” Jerome says “52.” What is the subtraction rule? Explain how you found your answer.

____

____

Use with text pages 116–118.

Name ______________________ Date ____________

Practice 5.5

Regroup Tens and Hundreds

Subtract. Check by adding.

1. 347 − 168
2. 568 − 289
3. 869 − 489
4. 582 − 194
5. 328 − 149
6. 543 − 345
7. 838 − 382
8. 726 − 436
9. 297 − 182 ______
10. 754 − 391 ______
11. 554 − 277 ______
12. 874 − 385 ______
13. 458 − 159 ______
14. $9.42 − $6.79 ______

Estimate by rounding. Then choose the correct answer.

15. 307 − 185
   a. 122 b. 222
16. 526 − 338
   a. 288 b. 188
17. 472 − 138
   a. 234 b. 334

Use mental math to compare. Write >, <, or = for each ◯.

18. 29 − 15 ◯ 54 + 5
19. 60 + 25 ◯ 60 − 50
20. 59 + 16 ◯ 88 − 13
21. 15 + 35 ◯ 79 − 29

22. A male grizzly bear weighs about 550 pounds. A female grizzly bear weighs about 285 pounds. How much more does the male grizzly bear weigh?

   A 265 pounds **C** 375 pounds
   B 365 pounds **D** 835 pounds

23. Jessica says that to find 519 − 239, you must regroup the hundreds place. Is she correct? Explain and show your work.

____
____
____
____

Use with text pages 120–122.

Name ______________________ Date ____________

Practice 5.6

Subtract Greater Numbers

Find each difference. Check by adding or estimating.

1. 5,737 − 2,565

2. 8,683 − 5,837

3. 6,398 − 2,520

4. 7,717 − 3,556

5. 8,647 − 6,488

6. $35.46 − $32.53

7. 9,428 − 5,149

8. 8,861 − 6,675

9. 7,896 − 5,603

10. 2,738 − 1,466

11. 4,635 − 2,829

12. 5,768 − 2,846

13. 3,548 − 1,459

14. 7,866 − 4,643

15. 6,437 − 4,821

16. 9,927 − 6,785

Mental Math Look for a pattern to subtract these numbers.

17. 8 − 5 = ■
80 − 50 = ■
800 − 500 = ■
8,000 − 5,000 = ■

18. 9 − 2 = ■
90 − 20 = ■
900 − 200 = ■
9,000 − 2,000 = ■

19. 4 − 1 = ■
40 − 10 = ■
400 − 100 = ■
4,000 − 1,000 = ■

Test Prep

20. Mr. Donaldson's company has 3,234 computers. He is having 1,307 of the computers serviced this month. How many computers at Mr. Donaldson's company are NOT being serviced?

A 2,937 **C** 2,927

B 1,937 **D** 1,927

21. Mr. Ruiz has 5,293 bees in his beehives. Mr. Andre has 2,565 bees in his beehives. Who has more bees? How many more? Explain how you found your answers.

____

____

Use with text pages 124–126.

Name ______________________ Date ____________

Practice 5.7

Subtract Across Zeros

Subtract. Check by adding or estimating.

1. 740 − 518

2. 600 − 358

3. 4,406 − 2,177

4. 900 − 535

5. 307 − 124

6. 860 − 424

7. 308 − 263

8. 8,007 − 6,352

9. 500 − 147

10. 300 − 162

11. 407 − 186 ______

12. 5,500 − 3,217 ______

13. 200 − 156 ______

14. 9,002 − 2,890 ______

15. 808 − 211 ______

16. 308 − 104 ______

17. 310 − 102 ______

18. 502 − 117 ______

19. 6,709 − 3,478 ______

Test Prep

20. A number, when subtracted from 900, leaves a difference of 637. What is the number?

A 263 **C** 1,437

B 363 **D** 1,537

21. Central Elementary School sold raffle tickets at the Spring Fair. The third grade sold 2,400 tickets. The fourth grade sold 1,276 tickets. How many more tickets did the third grade sell? Explain how you found your answer.

____

____

____

Use with text pages 128–129.

Name ______________________ Date ______________

Practice 5.8

Problem-Solving Decision: Explain Your Answer

Solve. Explain how you solved each problem.

Show your work.

1. Elizabeth and Tara both play on the girls' softball team. This season, Elizabeth has had 312 hits. Tara has had 176 hits. Who has had the greater number of hits? How many more hits has this person had?

____

____

____

2. The Romano family traveled 156 miles the first day of their trip, 180 miles the second day of their trip, and 154 miles the third day of their trip. How many miles did the Romano family travel on their three-day trip?

____

____

____

3. Bryan had $57.63. He bought a shirt for $26.59, including tax. How much money does Bryan have left?

____

____

____

Use with text page 130.

Name ______________________ Date ____________

Practice 6.1

Collect and Organize Data

Use the tally chart below for Questions 1–5.

Ways Students Get to School		
Way	**Tally**	**Number**
Walk	𝍸 III	8
Car	𝍸 I	6
Bus	𝍸 𝍸 𝍸	15
Bike	III	3

1. How many students were surveyed?

____

2. How many students ride in a car to get to school?

____

3. Which way is used by the fewest number of students to get to school?

____

4. Do more children walk or ride their bikes to school?

____

5. If you were to add a tally mark for the way you get to school how would the chart change?

____

Test Prep

6. The results of a survey of 12 children were as follows:

   1 child walks to school, 2 ride in a car, 1 rides a bike, and some children ride the bus.

   How many children ride the bus?

   A 6 **C** 5

   B 1 **D** 8

7. George surveyed 12 children. He listed his results in the tally chart below, but the tally marks for the children that ride the bus were erased! How many tally marks should there be for the children who ride the bus?

Ways Students Get to School	
Way	**Tally**
Walk	II
Car	II
Bus	
Bike	II

____

Use with text pages 148–149.

Name ______________________ Date ______________

Practice 6.2

Explore Range, Median, Mode, and Mean

The table below shows the number of players for each type of instrument.

Band Instruments	
Type of Instrument	**Number of Players**
tuba	3
drums	5
trumpet	7
clarinet	4
trombone	6
saxophone	2
flute	1

Use snap cubes to show the information above. Then use the cubes to answer Questions 1–5.

1. How many stacks of cubes are there?

____

2. What is the least number of cubes in a stack?

____

3. What is the greatest number of cubes in a stack?

____

4. What is the median? Explain what you did to find the median.

____

____

5. Draw a picture to show the mean. What is the mean?

Test Prep

6. What is the median of this group of numbers?

   0 2 4 6 8

   A 0 **C** 4

   B 8 **D** 6

7. If 0 people played the French horn, but it was added to the list of instruments, would the range of data or mode change? Explain your answer.

____

____

Name ______________________ Date ______________

Practice 6.5

Make a Pictograph

Use this pictograph to answer Questions 1–4.

Favorite Field Day Events	
Balloon Toss	🯅🯅🯅🯅🯅🯅
Obstacle Course	
100-yard Dash	🯅🯅🯅🯅🯅
Sack Race	🯅🯅🯅🯅🯅

Each 🯅 stands for 2 votes.

1. What is the title of the pictograph?

____

____

2. The obstacle course had 9 votes. Show this on the pictograph.

____

____

3. Which two events had the same number of votes?

____

____

4. Which event had the most votes?

____

____

Test Prep

5. Use the table at the right to complete the pictograph.

Favorite Tree	Number
Oak	
Pine	
Cypress	
Maple	

Each 🌲 stands for 4 votes.

Favorite Tree	Number
Oak	4
Pine	8
Cypress	12
Maple	2

6. Suppose 16 people voted for willow trees. How many symbols would you place next to willow tree?

A 4 C 16

B 8 D 2

Use with text pages 162–163.

Name ______________________ Date ____________

Practice 6.6

Make a Bar Graph

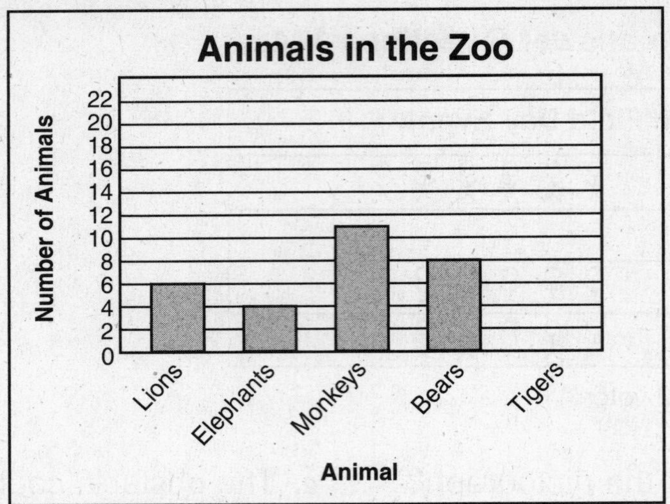

Use the bar graph for questions 1–7.

1. What does the graph show?

____

2. What is the scale of this graph?

____

3. There are 2 tigers in the zoo. Show that on the bar graph above.

____

4. Which animal is there the most of?

____

5. How many lions are in the zoo?

____

6. How many more monkeys are there than elephants?

____

Test Prep

7. When you add together the numbers of these two animals that are in the zoo, the sum is the same as the number of bears in the zoo.

   A elephants tigers
   B lions and tigers
   C elephants and monkeys
   D elephants and lions

8. Give an example of a set of data that you would use a bar graph to display.

____

Use with text pages 164–166.

Name ______________________ Date ____________

Practice 7.2

Identify Outcomes

The tally chart shows the results of tossing a cube 20 times. Complete the chart.

Color	Tally	Number
Purple	~~||||~~ ~~||||~~ ||	
Green	~~||||~~ |||	

Use the tally chart to answer Problems 1–4.

1. What are the two possible outcomes?

____

2. How many times did the cube land on the color purple?

____

3. How many times did the cube land on the color green?

____

4. What color are you least likely to land on?

____

Suppose you put these objects in a bag. Predict which object you are more likely to pull out.

5. 

____

6. 

____

7. 

____

8. 

____

Test Prep

9. If Danny puts 7 green marbles, 2 pink marbles, and 12 blue marbles in a box, which color marble is he most likely to pull out?

   A green   **C** pink

   B blue   **D** yellow

10. Lilly placed 5 oranges, 1 peach, and 2 apples in a bag. Which fruit is she least likely to pull out of the bag? Explain your reasoning.

____

____

Name ______________________ Date ____________

Practice 7.3

Outcomes and Probability

Write the probability of picking each letter.

PINEAPPLE

1. P ______

2. N ______

3. E ______

COCONUT

4. C ______

5. O ______

6. T ______

Write the probability of spinning each symbol.

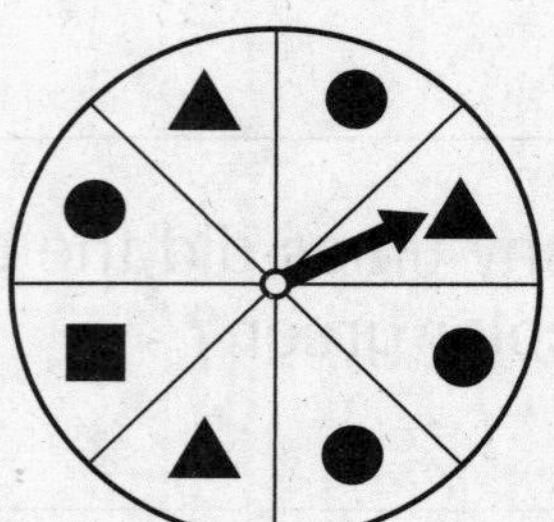

7. star ______

8. moon ______

9. sun ______

10. circle ______

11. triangle ______

12. square ______

Test Prep

13. An aquarium has 10 fish. Of the fish, 3 are blue, 5 are gold, and 2 are black. What is the probability of picking a blue fish?

A 1 out of 10

B 3 out of 10

C 2 out of 10

D 5 out of 10

14. On a cube, 1 side is green, 2 sides are yellow, and 3 sides are red. If the cube is tossed, which color is most likely to land facing up? Explain your reasoning.

____

____

____

Use with text pages 182–183.

Name ______________________ Date ____________

Practice 7.4

Make Predictions

Use the information below for Problems 1–2.

The graph shows the results of picking a bead from a bag 30 times. The bead was returned to the bag each time.

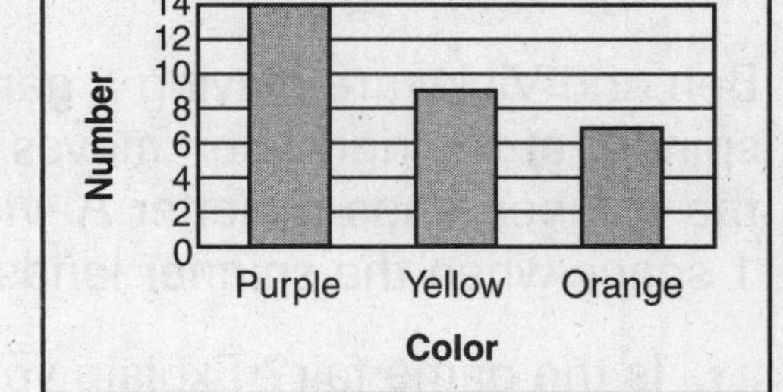

1. Predict the color of the next bead to be picked.

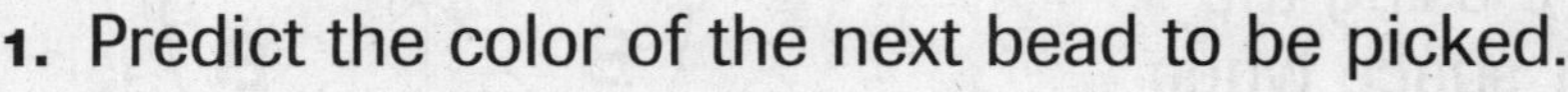

2. Predict the color bead that will least likely be picked.

____

Solve.

3. Look at the tally table. Which coin do you predict will be picked next?

____

Picking Coins From a Bag		
Outcome	**Tally**	**Number**
penny	|||	3
dime	~~||||~~ ||	7

Test Prep

4. Brice has 20 color markers in a bag. Of the markers, 5 are red, 8 are blue, 3 are yellow, and 4 are orange. He reaches into the bag and pulls out a marker. What color do you predict the marker will be?

   A red **C** blue

   B yellow **D** orange

5. Alisa put 7 green tiles, 5 blue tiles, and 2 red tiles in a bag. Predict the color she is least likely to pull from the bag. Explain your reasoning.

____

____

____

____

Name ______________________ Date ______________

Practice 7.5

Problem-Solving Application: Use Probability

Use the information below for Problems 1–3.

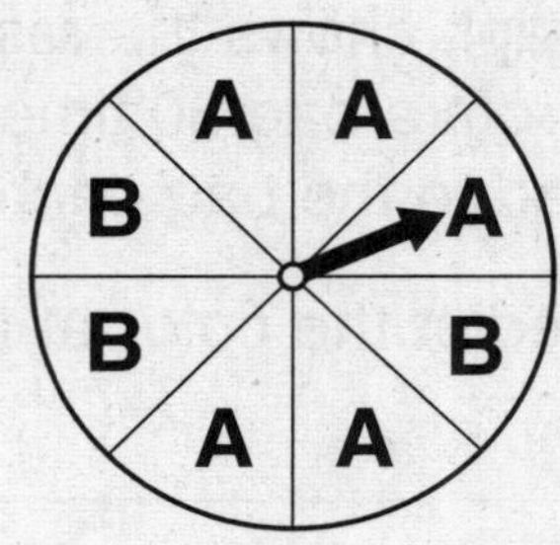

Ben and Vicky are playing a game using the spinner at the right. Ben moves 1 space when the spinner lands on letter A. Vicky moves 1 space when the spinner lands on letter B.

1. Is the game fair? Explain your answer.

____

2. Who is more likely to win? Explain your answer.

____

____

3. Draw another spinner Ben and Vicky could use to play a fair game.

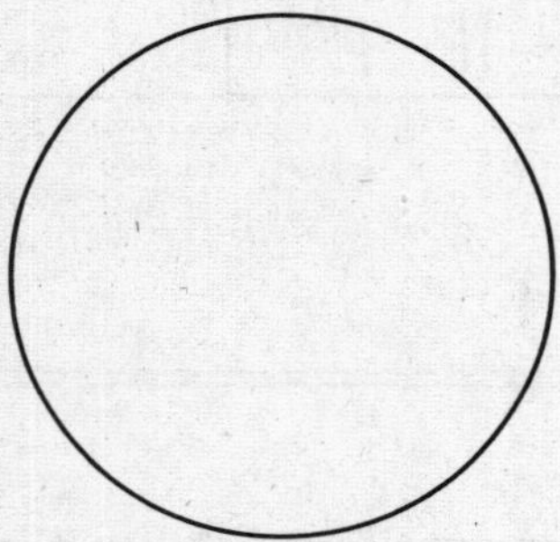

Write whether the game described below is *fair* or *unfair*. Explain your answer.

4. Rachael and Renee play a game with a number cube labeled 1–6. They take turns tossing the cube. Rachael gets 1 point for each odd number. Renee gets 1 point for each even number.

____

____

Use with text pages 188–189.

Name ______________________ Date ____________

Practice 8.1

Model Multiplication as Repeated Addition

Look at each group. Write an addition sentence and a multiplication sentence for each.

1.

____

____

2.

____

____

Model each set with counters. Then write an addition sentence and a multiplication sentence for each.

3. 6 groups of 2

____

____

4. 2 groups of 5

____

____

5. 3 groups of 3

____

____

6. 4 groups of 4

____

____

Write a multiplication sentence for each.

7. $2 + 2 + 2 = 6$

____

8. $4 + 4 = 8$

____

Test Prep

9. What is the correct multiplication sentence for $5 + 5 + 5 = 15$?

A $5 \times 2 = 10$ **C** $3 \times 5 = 15$

B $4 \times 3 = 12$ **D** $5 \times 5 = 25$

10. Write an addition sentence and a multiplication sentence for 4 groups of 5.

____

____

Use with text pages 206–207.

Name ______________________ Date ____________

Practice 8.2

Arrays and Multiplication

Write a multiplication sentence for each array.

1.

____

____

2.

____

____

3.

____

____

4.

____

____

Algebra • Properties Find each missing number.

5. $2 \times 6 = 12$
   $6 \times 2 = \blacksquare$

6. $7 \times 4 = 28$
   $\blacksquare \times 7 = 28$

7. $5 \times 4 = 20$
   $4 \times \blacksquare = 20$

8. $45 = 9 \times 5$
   $\blacksquare = 5 \times 9$

9. $8 \times 6 = 48$
   $6 \times 8 = \blacksquare$

10. $3 \times 4 = 12$
    $4 \times \blacksquare = 12$

11. $7 \times 6 = 42$
    $\blacksquare \times 7 = 42$

12. $24 = 3 \times 8$
    $\blacksquare = 8 \times 3$

Test Prep

13. Which number should be placed in the box to make the sentence true?

    $4 \times 9 = \blacksquare \times 4$

    A 8 **C** 9

    B 6 **D** 36

14. Draw arrays that show 2×7 is the same as 7×2. Find the product.

____

____

____

Use with text pages 208–209.

Name ______________________ Date ______________

Practice 8.3

Multiply With 2

Write a multiplication sentence for each picture.

1.

____

2.

____

3.

____

Multiply.

4. $\begin{array}{r} 2 \\ \times 2 \\ \hline \end{array}$	**5.** $\begin{array}{r} 5 \\ \times 2 \\ \hline \end{array}$	**6.** $\begin{array}{r} 4 \\ \times 2 \\ \hline \end{array}$	**7.** $\begin{array}{r} 7 \\ \times 2 \\ \hline \end{array}$	**8.** $\begin{array}{r} 1 \\ \times 2 \\ \hline \end{array}$	**9.** $\begin{array}{r} 9 \\ \times 2 \\ \hline \end{array}$
10. $\begin{array}{r} 3 \\ \times 2 \\ \hline \end{array}$	**11.** $\begin{array}{r} 2 \\ \times 7 \\ \hline \end{array}$	**12.** $\begin{array}{r} 2 \\ \times 6 \\ \hline \end{array}$	**13.** $\begin{array}{r} 10 \\ \times 2 \\ \hline \end{array}$	**14.** $\begin{array}{r} 2 \\ \times 8 \\ \hline \end{array}$	**15.** $\begin{array}{r} 5 \\ \times 2 \\ \hline \end{array}$
16. $\begin{array}{r} 2 \\ \times 9 \\ \hline \end{array}$	**17.** $\begin{array}{r} 2 \\ \times 3 \\ \hline \end{array}$	**18.** $\begin{array}{r} 6 \\ \times 2 \\ \hline \end{array}$	**19.** $\begin{array}{r} 2 \\ \times 4 \\ \hline \end{array}$	**20.** $\begin{array}{r} 8 \\ \times 2 \\ \hline \end{array}$	**21.** $\begin{array}{r} 2 \\ \times 1 \\ \hline \end{array}$

22. 2×10 ______ **23.** 2×4 ______ **24.** 2×6 ______ **25.** 2×9 ______ **26.** 3×2 ______

27. 4×2 ______ **28.** 2×7 ______ **29.** 1×2 ______ **30.** 2×2 ______ **31.** 8×2 ______

Test Prep

32. Ray has 8 football cards. John has 2 times as many cards as Ray. How many cards does John have?

A 12 cards **C** 14 cards

B 16 cards **D** 18 cards

33. Casey bought 3 boxes of candy. Each box cost \$2. How much did the candy cost altogether?

____

Use with text pages 210–211.

Name ______________________ Date ______________

Practice 8.4

Multiply With 4

Write a multiplication sentence for each picture.

1. 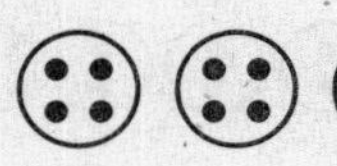

____

2. 

____

3. 

____

Find each product.

4. $\begin{array}{r} 8 \\ \times 4 \\ \hline \end{array}$

5. $\begin{array}{r} 7 \\ \times 4 \\ \hline \end{array}$

6. $\begin{array}{r} 4 \\ \times 5 \\ \hline \end{array}$

7. $\begin{array}{r} 1 \\ \times 4 \\ \hline \end{array}$

8. $\begin{array}{r} 4 \\ \times 8 \\ \hline \end{array}$

9. $\begin{array}{r} 4 \\ \times 3 \\ \hline \end{array}$

10. $\begin{array}{r} 6 \\ \times 4 \\ \hline \end{array}$

11. $\begin{array}{r} 9 \\ \times 4 \\ \hline \end{array}$

12. $\begin{array}{r} 4 \\ \times 4 \\ \hline \end{array}$

13. $\begin{array}{r} 10 \\ \times 4 \\ \hline \end{array}$

14. $\begin{array}{r} 4 \\ \times 7 \\ \hline \end{array}$

15. $\begin{array}{r} 4 \\ \times 9 \\ \hline \end{array}$

16. 4×2 ______

17. 7×2 ______

18. 4×4 ______

19. 2×5 ______

20. 2×8 ______

21. 6×4 ______

22. 9×2 ______

23. 8×4 ______

Algebra • Properties Find each missing number.

24. $2 \times 4 = \blacksquare$
$\blacksquare \times 2 = 8$

25. $5 \times 4 = \blacksquare$
$4 \times \blacksquare = 20$

26. $\blacksquare = 10 \times 4$
$40 = 4 \times \blacksquare$

27. $9 \times 2 = \blacksquare$
$2 \times \blacksquare = 18$

28. $\blacksquare = 4 \times 9$
$36 = 9 \times \blacksquare$

29. $2 \times 8 = \blacksquare$
$\blacksquare \times 2 = 16$

30. What is the product of 4×9?

A 32 C 33

B 35 D 36

31. A rabbit has 4 legs. How many legs do 5 rabbits have?

____

Use with text pages 212–214.

Name ______________________ Date ____________

Practice 8.5

Multiply With 5

Find each product.

1. 5×9 2. 2×5 3. 4×5 4. 7×5 5. 10×5 6. 3×5

7. 5×1 8. 6×5 9. 5×6 10. 5×10 11. 8×5 12. 2×5

13. 9×5 14. 5×5 15. 5×4 16. 5×8 17. 1×5 18. 5×7

19. 5×2 ____ 20. 5×4 ____ 21. 5×1 ____ 22. 6×5 ____ 23. 5×10 ____

24. 5×3 ____ 25. 7×5 ____ 26. 5×9 ____ 27. 8×5 ____ 28. 5×5 ____

Algebra • Equations Find each missing factor.

29. $5 \times ■ = 15$ 30. $■ \times 5 = 40$ 31. $10 = ■ \times 5$ 32. $■ \times 5 = 20$

33. $■ \times 5 = 35$ 34. $5 \times ■ = 45$ 35. $25 = 5 \times ■$ 36. $5 \times ■ = 10$

Test Prep

37. Kate puts 5 lightbulbs in each of 6 boxes. She has 4 lightbulbs left over. How many light bulbs does Kate have?

A 29 lightbulbs **C** 30 lightbulbs

B 34 lightbulbs **D** 35 lightbulbs

38. If you know the product of 6 and 5, how can you use it to find 7×5? Explain your answer.

____

____

____

____

Use with text pages 216–217.

Name ______________________ Date ____________

Practice 8.6

Multiply With 10

Find each product.

1. 2 ×10

2. 5 ×10

3. 4 ×10

4. 6 ×10

5. 3 ×10

6. 6 ×10

7. 8 ×10

8. 1 ×10

9. 10 ×10

10. 7 ×10

11. 9 ×10

12. 8 ×10

13. 10 × 7 ______

14. 10 × 4 ______

15. 10 × 3 ______

16. 10 × 2 ______

17. 10 × 10 ______

18. 10 × 9 ______

19. 10 × 7 ______

20. 10 × 6 ______

21. 10 × 1 ______

22. 10 × 5 ______

Algebra • Functions Complete each table by following the rule.

	Rule: Multiply by 10	
	Input	**Output**
23.	3	
24.		60
25.		50

	Rule: Multiply by 5	
	Input	**Output**
26.	3	
27.		25
28.	6	

	Rule: Multiply by 4	
	Input	**Output**
29.		16
30.	3	
31.		36

Test Prep

32. Find the product of 10 × 10.

A 1 **C** 10

B 100 **D** 1,000

33. Brett put books on shelves in the library. He put 10 books on each shelf. Brett completely filled 6 shelves with books. How many books did Brett put on shelves?

____

Use with text pages 218–219.

Name ______________________ Date ____________

Practice 8.7

Problem-Solving Strategy: Make an Organized List

Make an organized list to solve each problem.

Show your work.

1. Don is setting up a birdfeeder in his backyard. He can buy either a large feeder or a small feeder. He can fill the feeder with either mixed seeds or sunflower seeds. How many different ways could Don set up a birdfeeder?

____

2. Adam has a red shirt, a blue shirt, and a white shirt. He also has a brown pair, a black pair, and a blue pair of shorts. How many different ways can he wear one shirt and one pair of shorts?

____

3. Cathy is ordering a scoop of ice cream. She can order a cup, a sugar cone, or a waffle cone. The ice cream flavors are vanilla, peach, strawberry, mint, and chocolate. How many different combinations can Cathy order?

____

4. Karen won the poster contest at school. She got to choose either a radio or a CD player as her prize. Each prize comes in black, red, or green. How many choices does Karen have?

____

Name ______________________ Date ____________

Practice 8.8

Multiply With 1 and 0

Multiply.

1. $\begin{array}{r} 1 \\ \times 6 \\ \hline \end{array}$
2. $\begin{array}{r} 0 \\ \times 7 \\ \hline \end{array}$
3. $\begin{array}{r} 1 \\ \times 0 \\ \hline \end{array}$
4. $\begin{array}{r} 1 \\ \times 7 \\ \hline \end{array}$
5. $\begin{array}{r} 3 \\ \times 1 \\ \hline \end{array}$
6. $\begin{array}{r} 3 \\ \times 0 \\ \hline \end{array}$
7. $\begin{array}{r} 1 \\ \times 1 \\ \hline \end{array}$
8. $\begin{array}{r} 5 \\ \times 1 \\ \hline \end{array}$
9. $\begin{array}{r} 10 \\ \times 1 \\ \hline \end{array}$
10. $\begin{array}{r} 6 \\ \times 0 \\ \hline \end{array}$
11. $\begin{array}{r} 1 \\ \times 2 \\ \hline \end{array}$
12. $\begin{array}{r} 5 \\ \times 0 \\ \hline \end{array}$
13. $\begin{array}{r} 8 \\ \times 0 \\ \hline \end{array}$
14. $\begin{array}{r} 1 \\ \times 8 \\ \hline \end{array}$
15. $\begin{array}{r} 4 \\ \times 1 \\ \hline \end{array}$
16. $\begin{array}{r} 1 \\ \times 9 \\ \hline \end{array}$
17. $\begin{array}{r} 0 \\ \times 4 \\ \hline \end{array}$
18. $\begin{array}{r} 0 \\ \times 2 \\ \hline \end{array}$

19. 3×0 ______
20. 0×9 ______
21. 1×5 ______
22. 1×6 ______
23. 1×1 ______
24. 2×0 ______
25. 10×0 ______
26. 1×9 ______
27. 9×0 ______
28. 4×1 ______

Algebra • Properties Find each missing number.

29. $7 \times 1 = ■ \times 7$
30. $5 \times ■ = 0$
31. $8 \times 0 = ■ \times 8$
32. $4 \times ■ = 4$
33. $9 \times 0 = ■ \times 9$
34. $3 \times 1 = 1 \times ■$
35. $2 \times 2 = ■ \times 4$
36. $3 \times 3 = 1 \times ■$
37. $2 \times 4 = ■ \times 8$

Test Prep

38. Marbles are sold in bags of 10. Manny bought zero bags of marbles. How many marbles did Manny buy?

   A 0 marbles
   C 10 marbles
   B 20 marbles
   D 60 marbles

39. What is the product of any number and 1?

   ____

Use with text pages 224–226.

Name ______________________ Date ____________

Practice 9.1

Use a Multiplication Table

Below are parts of a multiplication table. In which row or column is each part found?

1.

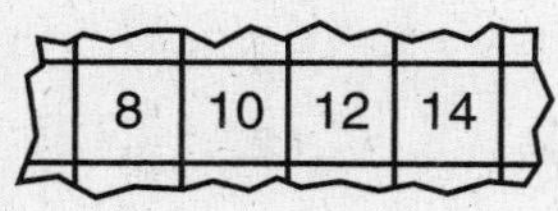

8	10	12	14

____

2.

18
27
36
45

____

3.

24	28	32	36

____

Write *true* or *false* for each statement. Give examples to support your answers.

4. The products in the row for 6 are double the products in the row for 3.

____

____

5. The product 16 appears one time in the multiplication table.

____

____

Test Prep

6. Which digits are in the ones place of a number multiplied by 5?

A 0 or 1 **C** 2 or 4

B 0 or 5 **D** 2 or 5

7. How could you use the products in the column for 1 to help you find the products in the column for 10?

____

____

____

____

Use with text pages 232–233.

Name ______________________ Date ____________

Practice 9.2

Multiply With 3

Find each product.

1. 3×4 = ____
2. 5×3 = ____
3. 3×0 = ____
4. 6×3 = ____
5. 3×3 = ____
6. 3×9 = ____
7. 8×3 = ____
8. 3×1 = ____
9. 7×3 = ____
10. 10×3 = ____
11. 4×3 = ____
12. 3×2 = ____

Draw an array for each. Then complete each multiplication sentence.

13. $3 \times 3 =$ ______
14. $1 \times 3 =$ ______
15. $3 \times 5 =$ ______
16. $3 \times 10 =$ ______
17. $2 \times 3 =$ ______
18. $6 \times 3 =$ ______

Test Prep

19. Choose the multiplication sentence that describes the array.

A $3 \times 6 = 18$

B $3 \times 7 = 21$

C $2 \times 7 = 14$

D $3 \times 8 = 24$

20. James is making omelets. Each omelet is made from 2 eggs. How many eggs are in 6 omelets?

____

Use with text pages 234–235.

Name ______________________ Date ____________

Practice 9.3

Multiply With 6

Find each product.

1. 6×2 **2.** 5×6 **3.** 10×6 **4.** 6×1 **5.** 6×3 **6.** 6×8

7. $6 \times 8 =$ ______ **8.** $6 \times 10 =$ ______ **9.** $1 \times 6 =$ ______

Algebra • Functions Complete each table.

	Rule: Multiply by 6	
	Input	Output
10.	7	
11.		24
12.		54
13.	2	

	Rule: Multiply by 3	
	Input	Output
14.	8	
15.		18
16.	10	
17.		15

Write *true* or *false.* If false, explain why.

18. Since $6 \times 3 = 18$, the product of 6×6 must be twice as much.

____

Algebra • Symbols Write >, <, or = for each ◯.

19. 3×6 ◯ 20 **20.** 25 ◯ 4×6 **21.** 36 ◯ 6×6

Test Prep

22. Mrs. Throneburg bought 7 packs of color pencils for her art class. Each pack of color pencils cost $6, including tax. What was the total cost of Mrs. Throneburg's purchase?

A $36 **C** $42

B $48 **D** $56

23. Mason works at a florist's shop. He is making corsages. Each corsage is made from 6 rosebuds. How many rosebuds will Mason need to make 10 corsages?

____

Use with text pages 236–239.

Name ______________________ Date ____________

Practice 9.4

Multiply With 7

Find each product.

1. 7×4 = ____ **2.** 2×7 = ____ **3.** 3×7 = ____ **4.** 7×1 = ____ **5.** 7×6 = ____ **6.** 7×5 = ____

7. 0×7 = ____ **8.** 10×7 = ____ **9.** 7×7 = ____ **10.** 9×7 = ____ **11.** 7×2 = ____ **12.** 7×8 = ____

13. $7 \times 3 =$ ______ **14.** $7 \times 10 =$ ______ **15.** $6 \times 7 =$ ______

16. $7 \times 7 =$ ______ **17.** $5 \times 7 =$ ______ **18.** $7 \times 8 =$ ______

19. $2 \times 7 =$ ______ **20.** $1 \times 7 =$ ______ **21.** $7 \times 4 =$ ______

Algebra • Symbols
Compare. Write >, <, or = for each ◯.

22. 3×7 ◯ 7×2

23. 4×7 ◯ 5×7

24. 8×7 ◯ 7×8

25. 1×7 ◯ 7×0

26. 6×7 ◯ 6×8

27. 6×9 ◯ 7×9

Test Prep

28. Choose the addition sentence you can use to find the product of 3×7.

A $7 + 7 = 14$

B $7 + 7 + 7 = 21$

C $7 + 7 + 7 + 7 = 28$

D $7 + 7 + 7 + 7 + 7 = 35$

29. Lisa bought 6 packs of trading cards. Each pack contains 7 cards. How many trading cards did Lisa buy?

____

Use with text pages 240–241.

Name ______________________ Date ____________

Practice 9.5

Multiply With 8

Find each product.

1. 8×3 = ___ **2.** 7×8 = ___ **3.** 4×8 = ___ **4.** 8×6 = ___ **5.** 8×1 = ___ **6.** 8×5 = ___

7. 2×8 = ___ **8.** 8×8 = ___ **9.** 0×8 = ___ **10.** 9×8 = ___ **11.** 10×8 = ___ **12.** 8×4 = ___

13. $8 \times 5 =$ ______ **14.** $8 \times 2 =$ ______ **15.** $10 \times 8 =$ ______

16. $7 \times 8 =$ ______ **17.** $1 \times 8 =$ ______ **18.** $8 \times 8 =$ ______

Algebra • Functions Complete each table.

Rule: Multiply by 8

	Input	Output
19.	4	
20.		64
21.		48
22.	9	

Rule: Multiply by 7

	Input	Output
23.	4	
24.		56
25.	0	
26.		70

Test Prep

27. Choose the number that will make the multiplication sentence true.

______ $\times 8 = 40$

A 5 **C** 6

B 7 **D** 8

28. How can you use doubling to find the product of 8×8?

____

Use with text pages 242–244.

Name ______________________ Date ____________

Practice 9.6

Multiply With 9

Multiply.

1. $\begin{array}{r} 9 \\ \times 7 \\ \hline \end{array}$ **2.** $\begin{array}{r} 0 \\ \times 9 \\ \hline \end{array}$ **3.** $\begin{array}{r} 1 \\ \times 9 \\ \hline \end{array}$ **4.** $\begin{array}{r} 9 \\ \times 6 \\ \hline \end{array}$ **5.** $\begin{array}{r} 9 \\ \times 8 \\ \hline \end{array}$ **6.** $\begin{array}{r} 9 \\ \times 5 \\ \hline \end{array}$

7. $\begin{array}{r} 4 \\ \times 9 \\ \hline \end{array}$ **8.** $\begin{array}{r} 9 \\ \times 9 \\ \hline \end{array}$ **9.** $\begin{array}{r} 3 \\ \times 9 \\ \hline \end{array}$ **10.** $\begin{array}{r} 9 \\ \times 0 \\ \hline \end{array}$ **11.** $\begin{array}{r} 10 \\ \times 9 \\ \hline \end{array}$ **12.** $\begin{array}{r} 9 \\ \times 4 \\ \hline \end{array}$

13. $\begin{array}{r} 9 \\ \times 2 \\ \hline \end{array}$ **14.** $\begin{array}{r} 6 \\ \times 9 \\ \hline \end{array}$ **15.** $\begin{array}{r} 9 \\ \times 3 \\ \hline \end{array}$ **16.** $\begin{array}{r} 9 \\ \times 0 \\ \hline \end{array}$ **17.** $\begin{array}{r} 5 \\ \times 9 \\ \hline \end{array}$ **18.** $\begin{array}{r} 7 \\ \times 9 \\ \hline \end{array}$

19. 9 × 3 = ______ **20.** 9 × 6 = ______ **21.** 1 × 9 = ______

22. 9 × 9 = ______ **23.** 5 × 9 = ______ **24.** 9 × 2 = ______

Algebra • Equations Find each missing number.

25. 3 × 10 = ______ × 5 **26.** 7 × ______ = 4 × 7

27. 6 × 6 = 9 × ______ **28.** ______ × 2 = 7 × 0

29. 8 × 2 = ______ × 4 **30.** 6 × ______ = 2 × 9

Test Prep

31. Which is the product of 5 × 9?

A 45 **C** 54

B 59 **D** 63

32. Justin bought 9 sodas with a $20 bill. If each soda cost $2, how much change should he receive?

____

Use with text pages 246–249.

Name ______________________ Date ____________

Practice 9.7

Patterns on a Multiplication Table

Write *true* or *false* for each statement. Give an example to support each answer.

1. Any multiple of 8 is also a multiple of 4.

2. All square numbers are odd numbers.

Write whether each array shows a square number. If not, find the fewest squares that could be added to make it show a square number.

3. 

4. 

5. 

Test Prep

6. Choose the number that is NOT a multiple of 12.

   A 50
   C 60
   B 84
   D 108

7. Is 49 a square number? Explain how you know.

Name ______________________ Date ____________

Practice 9.8

Multiply Three Numbers

Find each product. Multiply factors in parentheses first.

1. $(4 \times 2) \times 7 =$ ____
2. $11 \times (6 \times 0) =$ ____
3. $(1 \times 9) \times 5 =$ ____
4. $(2 \times 3) \times 8 =$ ____
5. $9 \times (3 \times 3) =$ ____
6. $(2 \times 5) \times 4 =$ ____
7. $5 \times (3 \times 4) =$ ____
8. $(2 \times 4) \times 8 =$ ____
9. $7 \times (2 \times 6) =$ ____
10. $(8 \times 1) \times 4 =$ ____
11. $7 \times (0 \times 9) =$ ____
12. $5 \times (3 \times 2) =$ ____

Algebra • Properties Use the Associative Property to find each missing factor.

13. (____ $\times 2) \times 6 = 60$
14. $4 \times$ (____ $\times 3) = 48$
15. $(6 \times 2) \times$ ____ $= 72$
16. $(4 \times 2) \times$ ____ $= 0$
17. ____ $\times (8 \times 1) = 24$
18. $(5 \times$ ____$) \times 8 = 80$
19. $7 \times$ (____ $\times 3) = 42$
20. (____ $\times 3) \times 6 = 54$
21. $2 \times (2 \times$ ____$) = 24$
22. $(4 \times 2) \times$ ____ $= 16$
23. $3 \times$ (____ $\times 1) = 27$
24. $3 \times (3 \times$ ____$) = 36$

Test Prep

25. Choose the missing factor.

$(3 \times 3) \times$ ____ $= 36$

A 3
C 4
B 5
D 6

26. Which factors would you multiply first to find the product of $2 \times 5 \times 3$? Explain your reasoning.

____

____

____

____

____

Use with text pages 252–253.

Name ______________________ Date ____________

Practice 9.9

Problem-Solving Decision: Multistep Problems

Solve each problem.

Show your work.

1. Kaya pasted 3 rows of photos on each of 5 pages of her scrapbook. She put 2 photos in each row. How many photos are in Kaya's scrapbook?

   ____

2. Cora has 4 party invitations in her scrapbook. Dan has 3 times as many party invitations as Cora. How many more party invitations does Dan have than Cora?

   ____

3. John's vacation scrapbook has 2 times as many pages as his school scrapbook. There are 6 pages in John's school scrapbook. How many pages are in both of John's scrapbooks combined?

   ____

4. Lisa bought 3 scrapbooks for $3 each. She gave the sales clerk $10. How much change should Lisa get?

   ____

5. Members of the Scrapbook Club meet 2 days a week for 2 hours each day. How many hours will they meet in 6 weeks?

   ____

Use with text pages 254–255.

Name ______________________ Date ____________

Practice 10.1

The Meaning of Division

Use counters to find the number in each equal group. Then complete each division sentence.

	Number of Counters	Number of Equal Groups	Number in Each Group	Division Sentence
1.	8	2		8 ÷ 2 = ____
2.	20	4		20 ÷ 4 = ____

Use counters to find the number of equal groups. Then complete each division sentence.

	Number of Counters	Number of Equal Groups	Number in Each Group	Division Sentence
3.	24		6	24 ÷ 6 = ____
4.	27		3	27 ÷ 3 = ____

Write a division sentence to describe each picture.

5. 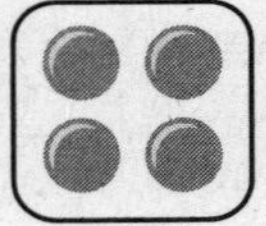 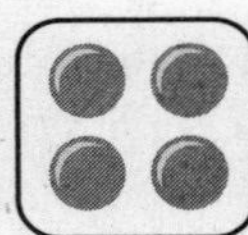 

____

6. 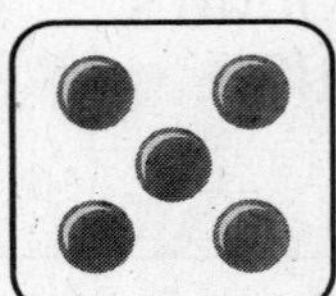 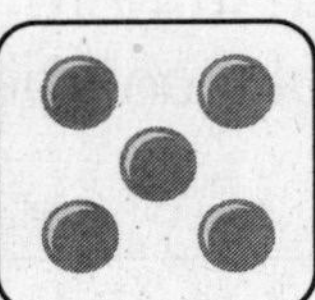

____

Test Prep

7. Choose the division sentence that models the picture.

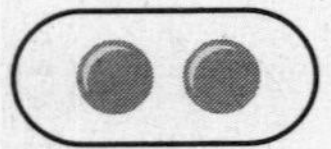 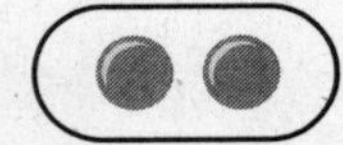

A 2 ÷ 2 = 1

B 6 ÷ 2 = 3

C 4 ÷ 2 = 2

D 4 ÷ 1 = 4

8. Describe two ways to divide 6 objects into equal groups.

____

____

Use with text pages 260–261.

Name ______________________ Date ____________

Practice 10.2

Model Division as Repeated Subtraction

Use repeated subtraction to find each quotient.

1. 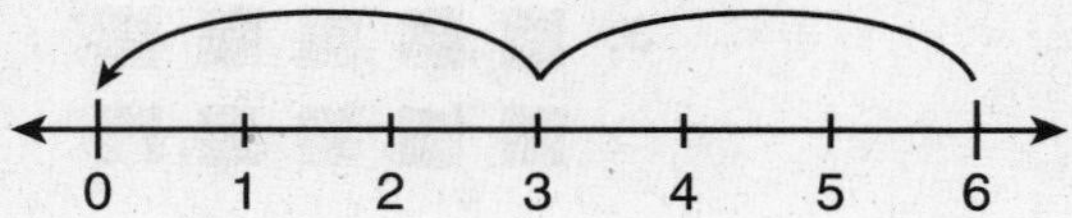

$6 \div 3 =$ ______

2. 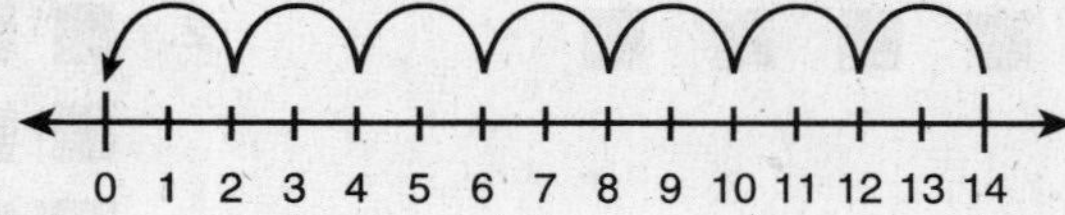

$14 \div 2 =$ ______

3. 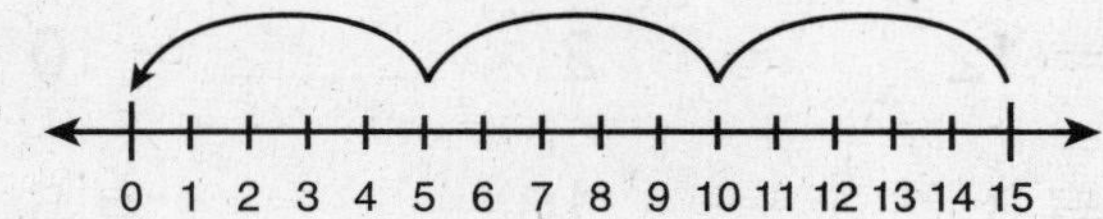

$15 \div 5 =$ ______

4. 

$18 \div 3 =$ ______

Match each number line with the correct division sentence. Solve.

5. ______ 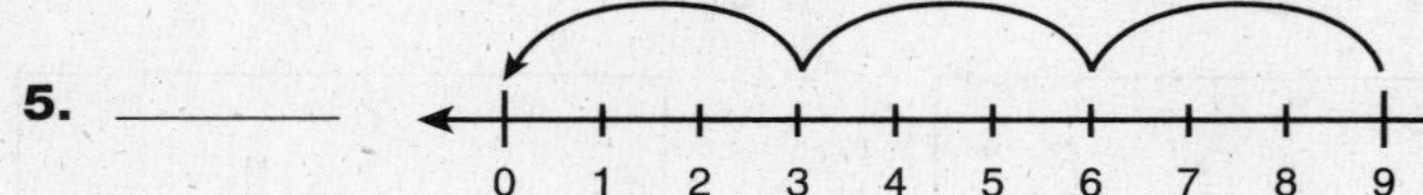

6. ______

7. ______

8. ______

a. $8 \div 2 =$ ______

b. $9 \div 3 =$ ______

c. $12 \div 6 =$ ______

d. $12 \div 3 =$ ______

Test Prep

9. Choose the division sentence that the number line shows.

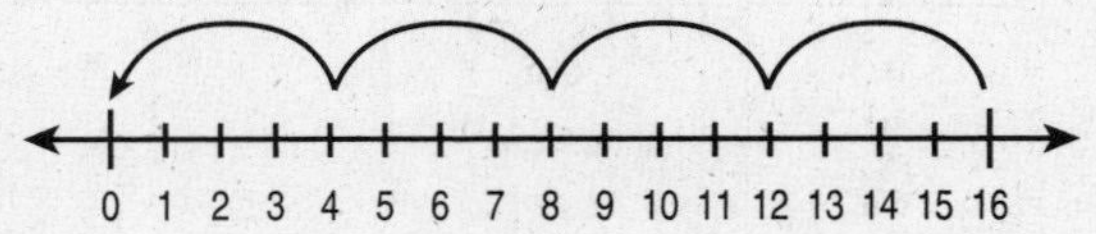

A $16 \div 16 = 1$

B $16 \div 4 = 4$

C $16 \div 8 = 2$

D $16 \div 2 = 8$

10. Describe how to show $10 \div 2 = 5$ on a number line.

____

____

____

Use with text pages 262–263.

Name ______________________ Date ______________

Practice 10.3

Relate Multiplication and Division

Use the array to complete each number sentence.

1\. ■ ■ ■ ■

$1 \times$ ______ $= 4$

$4 \div$ ______ $= 4$

2\. 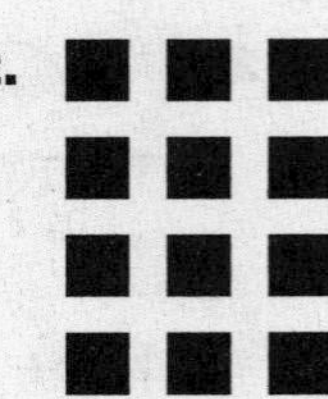

______ $\times 3 = 12$

______ $\div 4 = 3$

3\. ■ ■ ■ ■ ■
■ ■ ■ ■ ■

$2 \times$ ______ $= 10$

$10 \div$ ______ $= 5$

Draw an array for each multiplication sentence. Then write a related division sentence.

4\. $3 \times 2 = 6$

______

5\. $5 \times 1 = 5$

______

6\. $2 \times 6 = 12$

______

Test Prep

7\. Choose the multiplication and division sentences that the array shows.

A $2 \times 5 = 10$
$10 \div 5 = 2$

B $3 \times 4 = 12$
$12 \div 3 = 4$

C $3 \times 5 = 15$
$15 \div 3 = 5$

D $3 \times 6 = 18$
$18 \div 3 = 6$

8\. Make an array with 16 counters. Write the multiplication sentence and the division sentence that the array shows.

____

Use with text pages 264–265.

Name ______________________ Date __________

Practice 10.4

Divide by 2

Use the picture to find each quotient.

1. 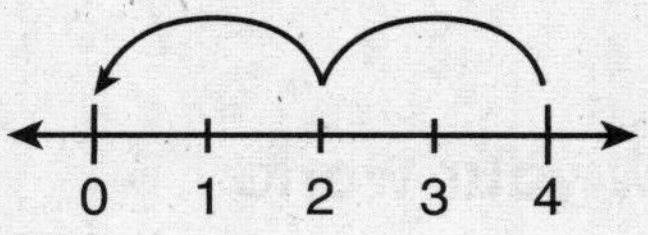

$4 \div 2 =$ ______

2. 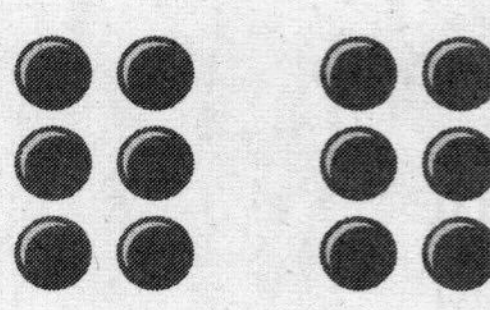

$12 \div 2 =$ ______

3. 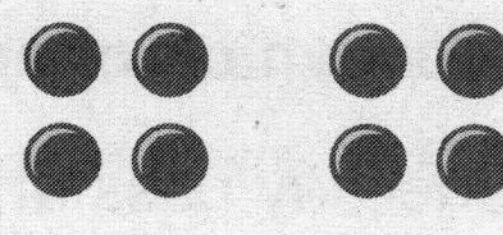

$8 \div 2 =$ ______

Use the multiplication fact to find each quotient.

4. $3 \times 2 = 6$

$6 \div 2$

______

5. $7 \times 2 = 14$

$14 \div 2$

______

6. $5 \times 2 = 10$

$10 \div 2$

______

7. $9 \times 2 = 18$

$18 \div 2$

______

8. $10 \times 2 = 20$

$20 \div 2$

______

9. $8 \times 2 = 16$

$16 \div 2$

______

10. $1 \times 2 = 2$

$2 \div 2$

______

11. $4 \times 2 = 8$

$8 \div 2$

______

Divide.

12. $2\overline{)18}$ **13.** $2\overline{)8}$ **14.** $2\overline{)10}$ **15.** $2\overline{)4}$ **16.** $2\overline{)20}$

17. $2\overline{)6}$ **18.** $2\overline{)14}$ **19.** $2\overline{)2}$ **20.** $2\overline{)16}$ **21.** $2\overline{)12}$

Test Prep

22. Choose the division sentence that the number line shows.

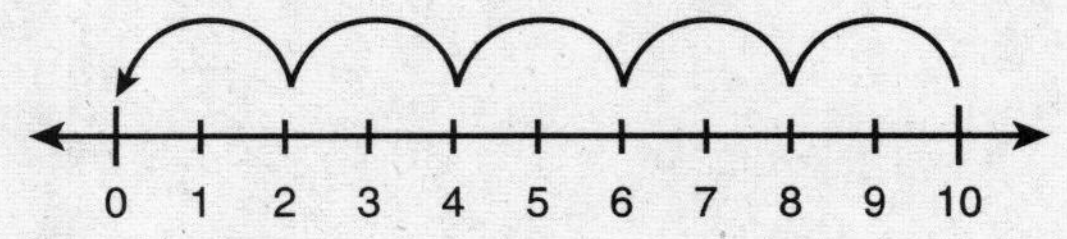

A $8 \div 2 = 4$ **C** $10 \div 2 = 5$

B $12 \div 2 = 6$ **D** $14 \div 2 = 7$

23. Ice-cream cones cost \$2 each. If Linda has \$12, how many ice-cream cones can she buy?

____

____

Use with text pages 266–267.

Name ______________________ Date ______________

Practice 10.5

Problem-Solving Decision: Choose the Operation

Solve. Tell which operation you used.

Show your work.

1. A one-day pass at an amusement park costs $10. How much would you pay for passes for yourself and a friend?

____

2. Twelve students are on a roller coaster. Two students are in each car. How many cars did the students fill?

____

3. Three hundred twenty-four students came to an amusement park on Friday. Five hundred seventeen students came on Saturday. What is the total number of students who came to the park on Friday and Saturday?

____

4. Jenna rode the merry-go-round 4 times. Each ride lasted 2 minutes. How many minutes did Jenna ride the merry-go-round in all?

____

5. Thirty-seven students were on the Ferris wheel. Eighteen students stayed on for another ride. How many students got off the Ferris wheel?

____

Use with text page 268.

Name ______________________ Date ______________

Practice 10.6

Divide by 5

Use the array to help you find the quotient.

1. 

15 ÷ 5 = ______

2.

35 ÷ 5 = ______

3.

20 ÷ 5 = ______

4. 

30 ÷ 5 = ______

5. 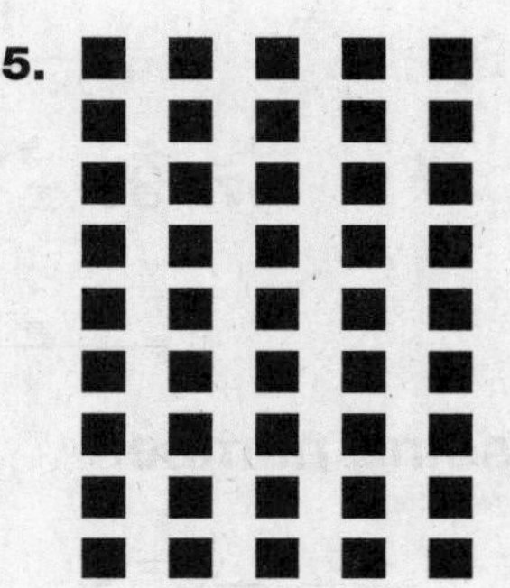

45 ÷ 5 = ______

6.

25 ÷ 5 = ______

Divide.

7. $5\overline{)50}$ **8.** $5\overline{)25}$ **9.** $2\overline{)14}$ **10.** $5\overline{)35}$ **11.** $2\overline{)20}$

12. $5\overline{)45}$ **13.** $5\overline{)20}$ **14.** $2\overline{)10}$ **15.** $5\overline{)5}$ **16.** $5\overline{)10}$

17. 15 ÷ 5 **18.** 16 ÷ 2 **19.** 40 ÷ 5 **20.** 30 ÷ 5 **21.** 20 ÷ 2

Test Prep

22. Choose the quotient.

45 ÷ 5 = ■

A 7 **C** 8

B 9 **D** 10

23. Heather has 20 pennies. She divides her pennies into 5 equal piles. How many pennies are in each pile?

____

Use with text pages 270–271.

Name ______________________ Date ____________

Practice 10.7

Divide by 10

Find each quotient.

1. $10\overline{)50}$ **2.** $10\overline{)80}$ **3.** $10\overline{)20}$ **4.** $10\overline{)60}$ **5.** $10\overline{)100}$

6. $10\overline{)30}$ **7.** $10\overline{)90}$ **8.** $10\overline{)70}$ **9.** $10\overline{)10}$ **10.** $10\overline{)40}$

11. $20 \div 10$ ______ **12.** $50 \div 10$ ______ **13.** $80 \div 10$ ______ **14.** $40 \div 10$ ______

15. $60 \div 10$ ______ **16.** $10 \div 10$ ______ **17.** $30 \div 10$ ______ **18.** $70 \div 10$ ______

Algebra • Equations Find each missing number.

19. $25 \div 5 =$ ______ **20.** $14 \div$ ______ $= 2$ **21.** ______ $\times 10 = 90$

22. $10 =$ ______ $\div 10$ **23.** $5 \times$ ______ $= 40$ **24.** $60 \div$ ______ $= 6$

25. $5 = 50 \div$ ______ **26.** $5 \times$ ______ $= 10$ **27.** ______ $\div 10 = 8$

Test Prep

28. Choose the quotient.

$70 \div 10 = \blacksquare$

A 4 **C** 5

B 6 **D** 7

29. Each pack of pencils contains 10 pencils. Allen has 60 pencils. How many packs of pencils does Allen have?

____

Use with text pages 272–273.

Name ______________________ Date ____________

Practice 10.8

Problem-Solving Strategy: Write a Number Sentence

Write a number sentence to solve each problem.

Show your work.

1. This year 250 more people came to a parade than last year. Last year 325 people attended the parade. How many people came to the parade this year?

   ____

2. There are 60 students in the marching band. There are 10 students in each row. How many rows of students are in the marching band?

   ____

3. A parade travels 2 miles on Elm Street, 1 mile on Washington Street, and 3 miles on Maple Street. How many miles did the parade travel?

   ____

4. There are 3 baseball teams in the parade. Each team has 9 players. How many baseball players are in the parade?

   ____

5. Students working at a parade refreshment stand earned $136 selling lemonade and $78 selling frozen yogurt. How much more money did the students earn selling lemonade than selling frozen yogurt?

   ____

Use with text pages 274–277.

Name ______________________ Date ____________

Practice 10.9

Algebra: Division Rules

Divide.

1. $5\overline{)25}$ **2.** $8\overline{)0}$ **3.** $2\overline{)8}$ **4.** $1\overline{)0}$ **5.** $1\overline{)10}$

6. $8\overline{)8}$ **7.** $10\overline{)40}$ **8.** $5\overline{)40}$ **9.** $6\overline{)6}$ **10.** $9\overline{)0}$

11. $1\overline{)4}$ **12.** $2\overline{)12}$ **13.** $10\overline{)80}$ **14.** $1\overline{)3}$ **15.** $2\overline{)16}$

16. $8 \div 1$ ______ **17.** $10 \div 10$ ______ **18.** $35 \div 5$ ______ **19.** $90 \div 10$ ______

20. $0 \div 10$ ______ **21.** $10 \div 2$ ______ **22.** $7 \div 7$ ______ **23.** $9 \div 1$ ______

24. $4 \div 4$ ______ **25.** $45 \div 5$ ______ **26.** $18 \div 2$ ______ **27.** $0 \div 9$ ______

Test Prep

28. Choose the division sentence that can be solved using this division rule: When any number is divided by 1, the quotient is that number.

A $486 \div 1 = n$ **C** $486 \div 486 = n$

B $0 \div 486 = n$ **D** $486 \div 2 = n$

29. Write three division sentences that can be solved using this division rule: When any number except 0 is divided by itself, the quotient is 1.

____

____

____

Use with text pages 278–281.

Name ______________________ Date ____________

Practice 11.1

Divide Using a Multiplication Table

Complete the chart. Use the multiplication table to help you.

	Example	Divisor	Dividend	Quotient
1.	42÷7			
2.	36÷6			
3.	24÷3			
4.	50÷5			

Use the multiplication table to find each quotient.

×	0	1	2	3	4	5	6	7	8	9	10
0	0	0	0	0	0	0	0	0	0	0	0
1	0	1	2	3	4	5	6	7	8	9	10
2	0	2	4	6	8	10	12	14	16	18	20
3	0	3	6	9	12	15	18	21	24	27	30
4	0	4	8	12	16	20	24	28	32	36	40
5	0	5	10	15	20	25	30	35	40	45	50
6	0	6	12	18	24	30	36	42	48	54	60
7	0	7	14	21	28	35	42	49	56	63	70
8	0	8	16	24	32	40	48	56	64	72	80
9	0	9	18	27	36	45	54	63	72	81	90
10	0	10	20	30	40	50	60	70	80	90	100

5. 18 ÷ 2 = ______ **6.** 45 ÷ 9 = ______

7. 15 ÷ 5 = ______ **8.** 7 ÷ 1 = ______

9. 32 ÷ 8 = ______ **10.** 32 ÷ 4 = ______

11. 10 ÷ 10 = ______ **12.** 12 ÷ 6 = ______

13. 70 ÷ 7 = ______ **14.** 27 ÷ 3 = ______

Test Prep

15. Choose the division sentence that has 9 as the dividend.

A 9 ÷ 3 = 3 **C** 27 ÷ 3 = 9

B 36 ÷ 9 = 4 **D** 18 ÷ 2 = 9

16. Find a number that appears more than once in the table. Use the number as a dividend in two division sentences.

____

____

____

____

Use with text pages 286–287.

Name ______________________________ Date ____________

Practice 11.2

Algebra: Fact Families

Complete each fact family.

1. 1 × 6 = 6

6 × ____ = 6

6 ÷ 1 = ____

6 ÷ ____ = 1

2. 4 × 7 = 28

____ × 4 = 28

28 ÷ ____ = 7

28 ÷ ____ = 4

3. 8 × 5 = 40

5 × ____ = 40

40 ÷ 5 = ____

____ ÷ 8 = 5

4. 3 × 9 = 27

9 × 3 = ____

____ ÷ 3 = 9

27 ÷ 9 = ____

Write a fact family for each set of numbers.

5. 2, 4, 8

6. 10, 6, 60

7. 5, 3, 15

8. 5, 5, 25

9. 8, 9, 72

10. 7, 6, 42

11. 1, 2, 2

12. 6, 5, 30

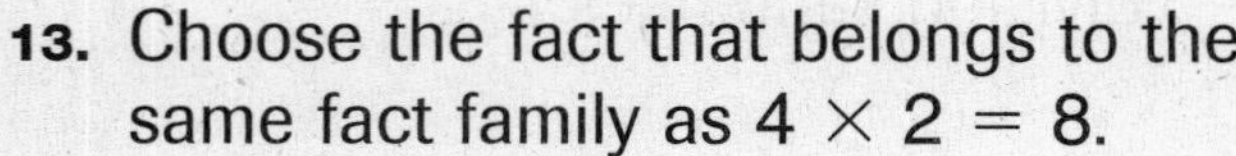

Test Prep

13. Choose the fact that belongs to the same fact family as 4 × 2 = 8.

A 2 × 2 = 4

B 4 ÷ 2 = 2

C 8 ÷ 2 = 4

D 1 × 8 = 8

14. Why do some fact families have only two facts? Give an example.

Use with text pages 288–289.

Name ______________________ Date ____________

Practice 11.3

Divide by 3

Divide.

1. $3\overline{)9}$ **2.** $3\overline{)24}$ **3.** $3\overline{)12}$ **4.** $3\overline{)21}$ **5.** $3\overline{)3}$

6. $3\overline{)15}$ **7.** $3\overline{)6}$ **8.** $3\overline{)0}$ **9.** $3\overline{)18}$ **10.** $3\overline{)27}$

11. $21 \div 3$ ______ **12.** $27 \div 3$ ______ **13.** $30 \div 3$ ______ **14.** $24 \div 3$ ______

15. $18 \div 3$ ______ **16.** $0 \div 3$ ______ **17.** $15 \div 3$ ______ **18.** $3 \div 3$ ______

Algebra • Symbols Write <, >, or = in each ◯.

19. 3×2 ◯ $12 \div 2$ **20.** 9×3 ◯ $9 + 3$ **21.** $30 \div 3$ ◯ $30 - 3$

22. 3×3 ◯ $18 \div 2$ **23.** $17 - 9$ ◯ 5×2 **24.** $21 \div 3$ ◯ 6×3

25. $3 - 3$ ◯ $3 \div 1$ **26.** $7 + 9$ ◯ $10 - 7$ **27.** $3 + 3$ ◯ 2×3

Test Prep

28. Choose the division sentence that the number line shows.

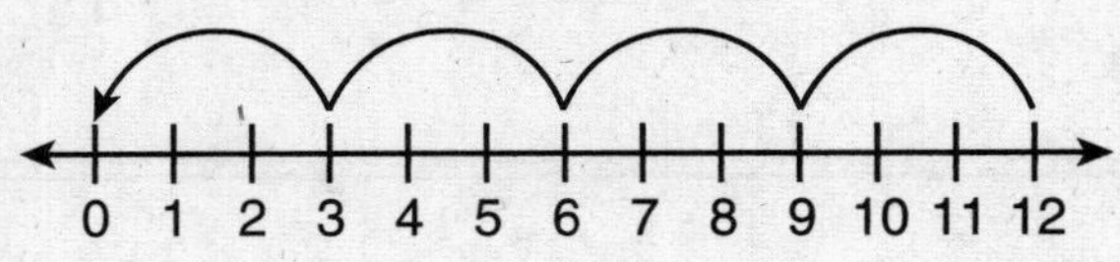

A $0 \div 3 = 0$ **C** $12 \div 3 = 4$

B $3 \div 3 = 1$ **D** $9 \div 3 = 3$

29. Thomas baked 24 cupcakes for the bake sale. The flavors of the cupcakes were yellow, white, and chocolate. Thomas baked the same number of each type of cupcake. How many chocolate cupcakes did he bake?

____

Name ______________________ Date ______________

Practice 11.4

Divide by 4

Find each factor and quotient.

1. 4 × ______ = 8

8 ÷ 4 = ______

2. 4 × ______ = 20

20 ÷ 4 = ______

3. 4 × ______ = 32

32 ÷ 4 = ______

4. 4 × ______ = 16

16 ÷ 4 = ______

5. 4 × ______ = 24

24 ÷ 4 = ______

6. 4 × ______ = 40

40 ÷ 4 = ______

Find the quotient.

7. $4\overline{)8}$ **8.** $4\overline{)20}$ **9.** $4\overline{)0}$ **10.** $4\overline{)36}$ **11.** $4\overline{)16}$

12. 28 ÷ 4 = ______ **13.** 12 ÷ 4 = ______ **14.** 4 ÷ 4 = ______

Algebra • Functions Complete each table. If the rule is not given, write the rule and complete the table.

	Rule: Divide by 4	
15.	36	
16.		7
17.	16	
18.		3

	Rule: Divide by 3	
19.	0	
20.		4
21.	18	
22.		9

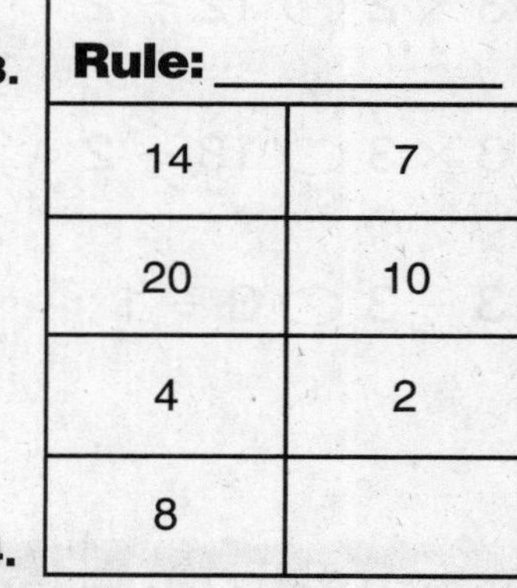

23.	Rule: ______	
	14	7
	20	10
	4	2
24.	8	

Use ÷ or × to complete each number sentence.

25. 4 ◯ 9 = 6 ◯ 6

26. 2 ◯ 4 = 32 ◯ 4

Test Prep

27. What is the quotient of twelve divided by four?

A 3 **C** 12

B 4 **D** 48

28. Can you divide 25 into 4 equal groups? Explain why or why not.

____

____

Use with text pages 292–294.

Name ______________________ Date ____________

Practice 11.5

Divide by 6

Find the quotient.

1. $6\overline{)18}$ **2.** $6\overline{)24}$ **3.** $6\overline{)6}$ **4.** $6\overline{)36}$ **5.** $6\overline{)30}$

6. $6\overline{)12}$ **7.** $6\overline{)60}$ **8.** $6\overline{)0}$ **9.** $6\overline{)48}$ **10.** $6\overline{)42}$

11. $30 \div 6 =$ ______ **12.** $48 \div 6 =$ ______ **13.** $18 \div 6 =$ ______

14. $6 \div 6 =$ ______ **15.** $54 \div 6 =$ ______ **16.** $36 \div 6 =$ ______

17. $60 \div 6 =$ ______ **18.** $42 \div 6 =$ ______ **19.** $24 \div 6 =$ ______

Algebra • Symbols. Write <, >, or = in each ◯.

20. $48 \div 6$ ◯ 9 **21.** $54 \div 6$ ◯ 8 **22.** $24 \div 3$ ◯ $42 \div 6$

23. 4×2 ◯ $16 \div 2$ **24.** 7 ◯ $32 \div 4$ **25.** 50 ◯ 5×9

26. $0 \div 3$ ◯ 3×0 **27.** $60 \div 10$ ◯ 10×6 **28.** 10 ◯ $27 \div 3$

Test Prep

29. Janet has 54 stickers in her album. Each page in the album has 6 stickers. How many pages are in Janet's sticker album?

A 6 **C** 9

B 8 **D** 10

30. Pete has 42 tomatoes to divide equally among his 6 friends. How many tomatoes did he give each friend?

____

Use with text pages 296–297.

Name ______________________________ Date ______________

Practice 11.6

Problem-Solving Strategy: Draw a Picture

Draw a picture to solve each problem.

Show your work.

1. A board is 54 inches long. Nate cuts the board into 6 equal pieces. How long is each piece?

   ____

2. Erin is cutting a loaf of bread into 12 slices. What is the fewest number of cuts she can make?

   ____

3. There are 24 flowers planted in a flower bed. The flowers are pink, yellow, white, and purple. Every fourth flower is pink. How many pink flowers are there?

   ____

4. There are 3 wagons in a wagon train. Each wagon is 15 feet long. There are 5 feet between each wagon. What is the length of the wagon train?

   ____

5. Pete's mom buys 48 inches of ribbon. First she cuts the ribbon in half. Then she cuts each piece into 3 equal pieces. How many pieces of ribbon will she have then?

   ____

Use with text pages 300–303.

Name ______________________ Date ______________

Practice 11.7

Divide by 7

Divide.

1. $7\overline{)35}$ 2. $7\overline{)49}$ 3. $7\overline{)14}$ 4. $7\overline{)70}$ 5. $7\overline{)0}$

6. $7\overline{)21}$ 7. $7\overline{)63}$ 8. $7\overline{)7}$ 9. $7\overline{)42}$ 10. $7\overline{)56}$

11. $28 \div 7 =$ ______ 12. $14 \div 7 =$ ______ 13. $63 \div 7 =$ ______

14. $7 \div 7 =$ ______ 15. $56 \div 7 =$ ______ 16. $49 \div 7 =$ ______

Algebra • Symbols. Write +, −, ×, or ÷ in each ○.

17. 28 ○ 7 = 4 18. 9 ○ 6 = 15 19. 18 ○ 9 = 9

20. 5 ○ 5 = 0 21. 35 ○ 7 = 5 22. 36 ○ 6 = 30

23. 8 ○ 4 = 32 24. 0 ○ 2 = 2 25. 9 ○ 4 = 36

Test Prep

26. The party store ordered 35 balloons in 7 different colors. If the same number of each color is ordered, how many of each color is ordered?

A 4 C 6

B 5 D 7

27. How could knowing that $35 \div 7 = 5$ help you find $42 \div 7$? Explain.

____

____

____

____

Use with text pages 304–305.

Name ______________________ Date ____________

Practice 11.8

Divide by 8

Divide.

1. $8\overline{)40}$ 2. $8\overline{)56}$ 3. $8\overline{)16}$ 4. $8\overline{)72}$ 5. $8\overline{)8}$

6. $8\overline{)24}$ 7. $8\overline{)0}$ 8. $8\overline{)32}$ 9. $8\overline{)48}$ 10. $8\overline{)64}$

11. $16 \div 8 =$ ______ 12. $80 \div 8 =$ ______ 13. $72 \div 8 =$ ______

14. $8 \div 8 =$ ______ 15. $64 \div 8 =$ ______ 16. $0 \div 8 =$ ______

Find each missing number.

17. $30 \div 6 = n$

    $n =$ ______

18. $4 \times b = 36$

    $b =$ ______

19. $40 \div 8 = a$

    $a =$ ______

20. $b \times 8 = 56$

    $b =$ ______

21. $42 \div a = 6$

    $a =$ ______

22. $n \div 10 = 8$

    $n =$ ______

23. $8 \times r = 64$

    $r =$ ______

24. $8 \div 8 = p$

    $p =$ ______

25. $48 \div t = 6$

    $t =$ ______

Test Prep

26. Each table in a restaurant seats 8 people. How many tables are needed to seat a party of 64 people?

    A 6 C 8

    B 7 D 9

27. Why is $40 \div 8$ less than $48 \div 8$?

    ____

    ____

    ____

    ____

    ____

Use with text pages 306–309.

Name ______________________ Date ____________

Divide by 9

Find each factor and quotient.

1. 9 × ______ = 18

   18 ÷ 9 = ______

2. 9 × ______ = 45

   45 ÷ 9 = ______

3. 9 × ______ = 63

   63 ÷ 9 = ______

Divide.

4. $9\overline{)0}$
5. $9\overline{)90}$
6. $9\overline{)54}$
7. $9\overline{)45}$
8. $9\overline{)72}$

9. 36 ÷ 9 ______
10. 81 ÷ 9 ______
11. 72 ÷ 9 ______
12. 45 ÷ 9 ______

Algebra • Functions Find the rule. Then complete each table.

13. **Rule:** ____________

	36	4
	54	6
	18	2
14.		7
15.	0	

16. **Rule:** ____________

	25	5
	35	7
	10	2
17.	50	
18.		4

19. **Rule:** ____________

	42	7
	30	5
	18	3
20.		9
21.	48	

Test Prep

22. Susan has 63 books to display in a bookcase. If she puts 9 books on each shelf, how many shelves will she fill?

    A 6
    B 7
    C 8
    D 9

23. Would you use equal groups, a related multiplication fact, or a related division fact to find the quotient of 54 ÷ 9? Explain.

    ____

    ____

Use with text pages 310–313.

Name ______________________ Date ____________

Practice 12.1

Hour, Half-Hour, Quarter-Hour

Describe each time in at least two ways.

1.

____

____

2.

____

____

Write each time using numbers.

3. fifteen minutes after seven

____

4. half past twelve

____

5. quarter to eight

____

6. quarter after ten

____

Choose the most reasonable time to start each activity.

7. eating breakfast
- **a.** 7:00 A.M.
- **b.** 7:00 P.M.

8. going to sleep
- **a.** 8:15 A.M.
- **b.** 8:15 P.M.

9. going to recess
- **a.** 1:30 A.M.
- **b.** 1:30 P.M.

10. Which time is quarter to five?

A 4:25 **C** 4:45

B 5:15 **D** 5:45

11. Which is closer to six o'clock: quarter after six or half past six? Explain your answer.

____

____

Use with text pages 330–331.

Name ______________________ Date ______________

Practice 12.2

Time to Five Minutes

Describe each time as minutes after an hour and minutes before an hour.

1. 

____

____

2. 

____

____

3. 

____

____

4. 

____

____

Test Prep

5. Which time is 40 minutes after 2?

   A 2:20 C 2:40

   B 3:20 D 3:40

6. The minute hand is pointing to 7 and the hour hand is pointing between 3 and 4. How many minutes before 4:00 is it? Explain how you know.

____

____

Use with text pages 332–333.

Name ______________________ Date ____________

Practice 12.3

Time to the Minute

Describe each time two ways.

1.

____

____

2.

____

____

3.

____

____

4.

____

____

Describe each time in words.

5. 8:14

____

6. 1:53

____

7. 4:26

____

8. 10:44

____

Test Prep

9. Which time is 3 minutes after 2?

A 2:03 **C** 2:30

B 3:02 **D** 3:20

10. Is 11:22 before or after 11:00? Explain how you know.

____

____

____

____

Use with text pages 334–335.

Name ________________________ Date ______________

Practice 12.4

Elapsed Time

Tell what time it will be.

1. in 20 minutes.

____

2. in 7 hours.

____

Write the time using numbers. Label each time A.M. or P.M.

3. 20 minutes before midnight

____

4. 6 hours before 2:30 P.M.

____

5. 2 hours after 11:00 A.M.

____

6. 5 minutes before noon

____

Look at each pair of times. Write how much time has passed.

7. Start: 9:05 A.M.
End: 9:55 A.M.

____

8. Start: 3:35 P.M.
End: 5:10 P.M.

____

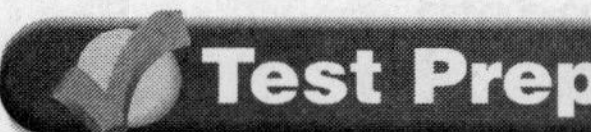

9. Choose the time it will be at 55 minutes after midnight.

A 11:05 A.M. C 12:55 A.M.

B 11:05 P.M. D 12:55 P.M.

10. Explain how to find the amount of time that has passed between 4:15 A.M. and 5:35 A.M.

____

____

____

____

Use with text pages 336–338.

Name ______________________ Date ____________

Practice 12.5

Use a Calendar

Use the July calendar for Exercises 1–3.

July						
Sun	**Mon**	**Tue**	**Wed**	**Thu**	**Fri**	**Sat**
		1	2	3	Picnic 4	5
6	7	8	9	10	11	Hiking Trip 12
13	14	15	16	17	18	19
20	21	22	23	24	25	26
27	28	29	30	31		

1. What date is the picnic?

____

2. What day of the week is July 22?

____

3. What is the date of the third Wednesday in July?

____

Name the month that is 5 months after each month.

4. May ____________

5. November ____________

6. January ____________

Name the month that is 4 months before each month.

7. June ____________

8. September ____________

9. December ____________

Name the date.

10. ninth day of the eleventh month ____________

11. twenty-third day of the fourth month ____________

12. second day of the first month ____________

13. Choose the date of the tenth day of the second month of the year.

A September 2

B February 10

C October 2

D March 10

14. Use the calendar above. What day of the week is the eighth of July? Explain how you know.

____

____

____

Use with text pages 340–342.

Name ______________________ Date ______________

Practice 12.6

Problem-Solving Application: Use a Schedule

Use the schedule below for Problems 1–4.

Summer Camp Schedule					
Activity	Canoeing	Hiking	Biking	Swimming	Fishing
Starting Time	9:00 A.M.	10:30 A.M.	12:00 P.M.	1:00 P.M.	1:00 P.M.
Ending Time	11:00 A.M.	11:30 A.M.	2:30 P.M.	3:20 P.M.	3:00 P.M.

Show your work.

1. Which activities start between 11:00 A.M. and 1:30 P.M.?

____

____

2. If the canoeing trip ends 30 minutes later than scheduled, would the campers who went on the trip still be able to go biking? Explain your answer.

____

____

3. Which activity starts at the same time as fishing but ends 20 minutes later?

____

4. Ingrid wants to go to activities that last more than 2 hours. Which activities should she choose?

____

Use with text pages 344–345.

Name ______________________ Date ____________

Practice 12.7

Temperature: Degrees Fahrenheit and Celsius

Write each temperature using °F or °C. Then write *hot*, *warm, cool,* or *cold* to describe the temperature.

1. 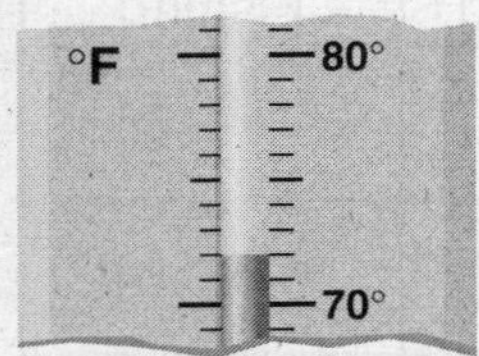

2. 

3. 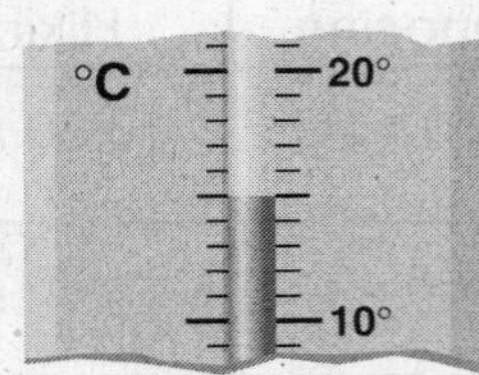

4. 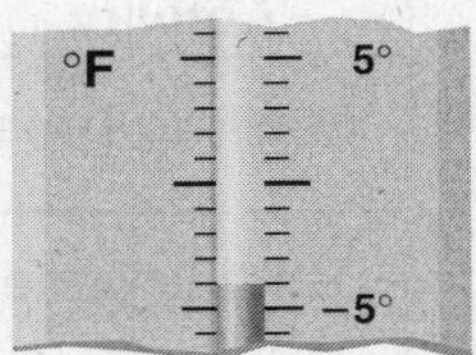

______ ______ ______ ______

______ ______ ______ ______

Write these temperatures in order from coldest to warmest.

5. 51°C, 88°C, 4°C ______

6. 21°F, 3°F, −10°F ______

7. 0°C, 0°F, 10°C ______

Choose the better estimate of the temperature.

8. 

a. 30°F
b. 92°F

9. 

a. −5°C
b. 28°C

10. 

a. 54°F
b. 0°F

11. Which word describes a temperature of 55°F?

A hot **C** warm

B cool **D** cold

12. Describe two activities you might do when the temperature is 30°C.

______

______

______

Use with text pages 346–348.

Name ______________________ Date ____________

Practice 13.1

Measure to the Nearest Inch

Estimate and then measure each object below to the nearest inch.

1\.

____

2\.

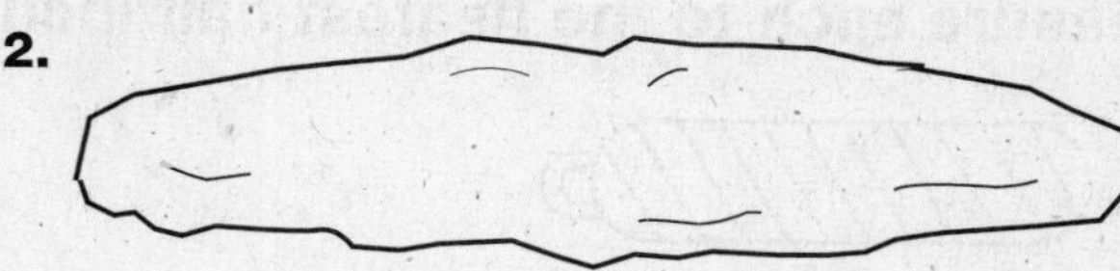

____

3\.

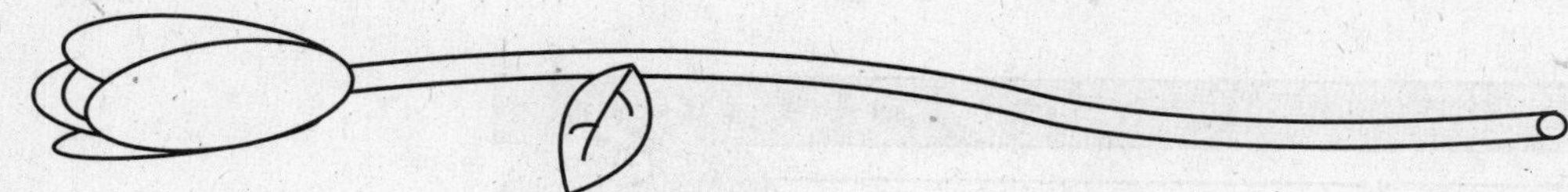

____

4\.

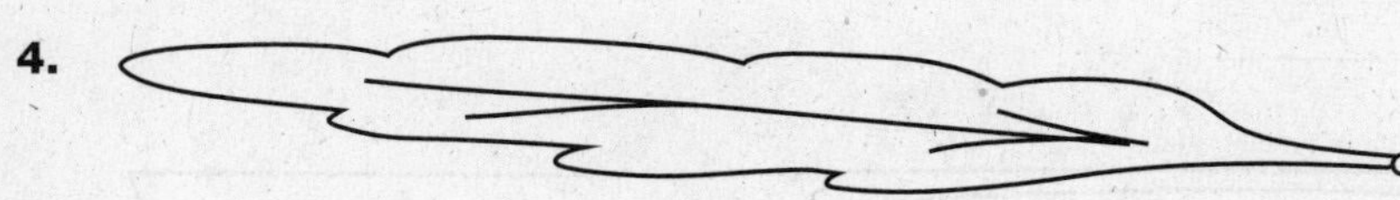

____

Use a ruler. Draw a line of each length.

5\. 4 inches

6\. 6 inches

7\. 1 inch

8\. Choose the best estimate.

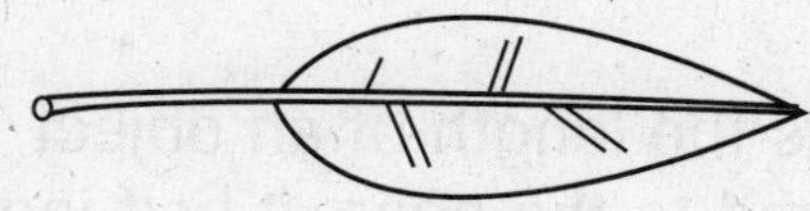

A about 2 inches **C** about 5 inches

B about 9 inches **D** about 11 inches

9\. When Jacob measured the length of a pencil, he lined up one end of the pencil with the number 1 on the ruler. The number closest to the other end of the pencil was 6. Jacob says the pencil is 6 inches long. What's wrong?

____

____

____

Use with text pages 354–357.

Name ______________________ Date ____________

Measure to the Nearest Half Inch

Measure each to the nearest half inch.

1. 

____

2. 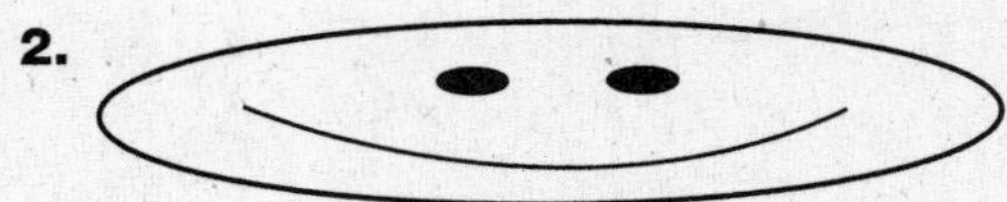

____

3. 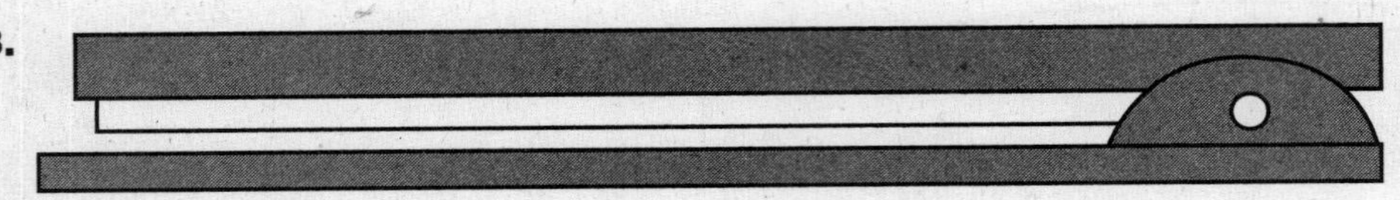

____

4. 

____

Use an inch ruler. Draw a line of each length.

5. $2\frac{1}{2}$ inches
6. 3 inches
7. $4\frac{1}{2}$ inches

Test Prep

8. Measure to the nearest half inch. Choose the length.

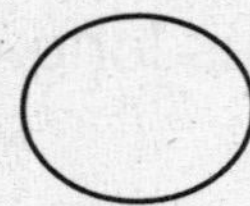

A $\frac{1}{2}$ inch
B $1\frac{1}{2}$ inches
C 1 inch
D 2 inches

9. When is the length of an object measured to the nearest half inch a whole number?

____

____

____

____

Name ______________________ Date __________

Practice 13.3

Customary Units of Length

Choose the better estimate.

1. the distance across a city

   a. 5 miles b. 5 feet

2. the width of a stamp

   a. 1 yard b. 1 inch

3. the length of a table

   a. 3 feet b. 3 miles

4. the height of a door

   a. 7 feet b. 7 inches

Complete.

5. 12 ft = ______ yd
6. 3 ft = ______ in.
7. 2 yd = ______ ft
8. 24 in. = ______ ft
9. 9 ft = ______ yd
10. 1 ft = ______ in.

Order from shortest to longest.

11. 48 in. 1 yd 2 ft

    ____

12. 20 mi 20 ft 20 yd

    ____

13. 5,000 ft 1 mi 2,000 yd

    ____

14. 4 yd 9 ft 72 in.

    ____

Test Prep

15. Choose the measurement that is greater than 3 feet.

    A 1 yard C 2 yards

    B 24 inches D 36 inches

16. Which is less, 3 feet or 48 inches? Explain how you know.

    ____

    ____

    ____

    ____

Use with text pages 360–362.

Name ______________________ Date ______________

Practice 13.4

Problem-Solving Strategy: Use Logical Reasoning

Use logical reasoning to solve each problem.

Show your work.

1. Bev, Carl, and Flora each have a seashell collection. The collections have 19, 26, and 35 shells. Carl has 9 fewer seashells than Flora. Carl has 7 more seashells than Bev does. How many seashells are in each person's collection?

____

____

2. Danny bought three stamps at a stamp show. The Canadian stamp cost $2 more than the Japanese stamp. The German stamp cost 3 times as much as the Canadian stamp. The Japanese stamp cost $7. What was the price of each stamp?

____

____

3. Hana, Joe, Cathy, and Abdul each bought a scrapbook. The scrapbooks cost $4, $6, $8, and $10. Joe's scrapbook cost $8. Hana's scrapbook cost less than Abdul's scrapbook. Cathy's scrapbook cost the most. How much did each of them pay for a scrapbook?

____

____

Use with text pages 364–366.

Name ______________________ Date ____________

Practice 13.5

Estimate and Measure Capacity

Use the chart to find the missing measure.

1 pint (pt) = 2 cups (c)

1 quart (qt) = 2 pints

1 gallon (gal) = 4 quarts

1. 4 qt = ______ pt **2.** 4 pt = ______ c

3. 4 gal = ______ qt **4.** 5 qt = ______ pt

5. 6 gal = ______ qt **6.** 1 gal = ______ pt **7.** 1 qt = ______ c

8. 3 pt = ______ c **9.** 2 qt = ______ c **10.** 3 gal = ______ pt

11. 2 gal = ______ pt **12.** 2 qt = ______ pt **13.** 4 qt = ______ c

Test Prep

14. How many quarts are in 5 gallons?

A 10 **C** 20

B 30 **D** 40

15. Ben says that he multiplied twice to find the number of cups in 3 quarts. Describe the steps that he used.

____

____

____

____

____

____

Use with text pages 368–369.

Name ______________________ Date __________

Practice 13.6

Customary Units of Capacity

Choose the unit you would use. Write *cup*, *pint*, *quart*, or *gallon*.

1. 

______

2. 

______

3. 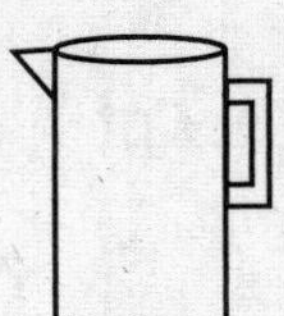
______

Choose the better estimate.

4. bath tub
   a. 40 gal b. 40 c

5. coffee mug
   a. 1 qt b. 1 c

6. bucket
   a. 3 c b. 3 qt

Write in order from least capacity to greatest capacity.

7. 2 quarts 3 pints 1 gallon
______

8. 1 pint 1 quart 3 cups
______

Complete.

9. 3 pt = ■ c

10. 2 c = ■ pt

11. 2 qt = ■ pt

 **Test Prep**

12. Which is equal to 6 cups?
   A 1 gallon
   B 2 quarts
   C 2 pints
   D 3 pints

13. Which unit would you use to measure the capacity of a swimming pool: cups or gallons? Explain.
______
______
______
______
______

Use with text pages 370–371.

Name ______________________ Date ____________

Customary Units of Weight

Choose the unit you would use to measure the weight. Write *ounce* or *pound.*

1. 

____

2. 

____

3. 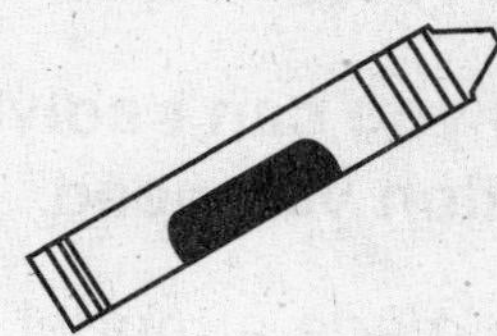

____

Choose the better estimate.

4. an apple

a. 3 oz **b.** 3 lb

5. a car

a. 2,000 oz **b.** 2,000 lb

6. a sock

a. 2 oz **b.** 200 oz

Write in order from the least weight to the greatest weight.

7. 25 oz 15 oz 1 lb

____

8. 35 oz 2 lb 30 oz

____

Find the missing measure.

9. 2 lb = ■ oz

10. 16 oz = ■ lb

11. $\frac{1}{2}$ lb = ■ oz

Test Prep

12. Choose the best estimate of the weight of a feather.

A 1 ounce

B 100 pounds

C 10 pounds

D 100 ounces

13. How many ounces are equal to 2 pounds? Explain how you know.

____

____

____

____

Use with text pages 372–374.

Name ______________________ Date ____________

Practice 13.8

Problem-Solving Decision: Too Much or Too Little Information

Solve. If you can't solve the problem, tell what information you need.

Show your work.

1. Julie made a model of a spaceship for the Science Fair. She worked for 2 hours each day making the model. How long did it take Julie to finish her project?

   ____

2. Jerome saved $15 to buy supplies for his science project. He paid $4.50 for paint, $3.65 for poster board, and $1.25 for markers. How much did he spend in all?

   ____

3. Rosa and Tom grew tomato plants for their science project. Rosa's plant grew 18 inches. How much more did Tom's plant grow than Rosa's plant?

   ____

4. The Science Fair starts at 9:00 A.M. and ends at 4:00 P.M. How long does the fair last?

   ____

Use with text page 376.

Name ______________________ Date ____________

Practice 14.1

Centimeter and Millimeter

Estimate. Then measure to the nearest centimeter.

1. 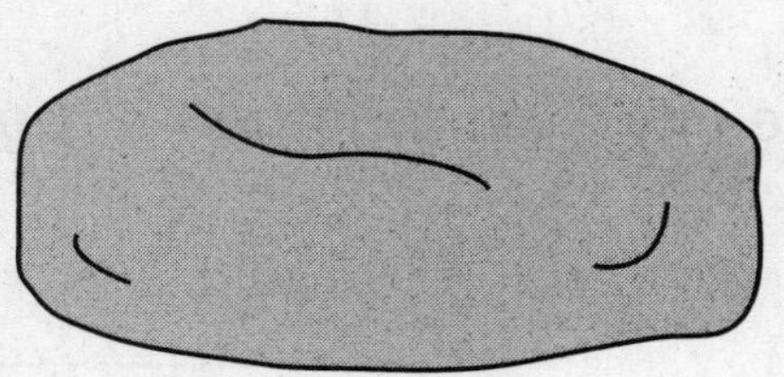

2. 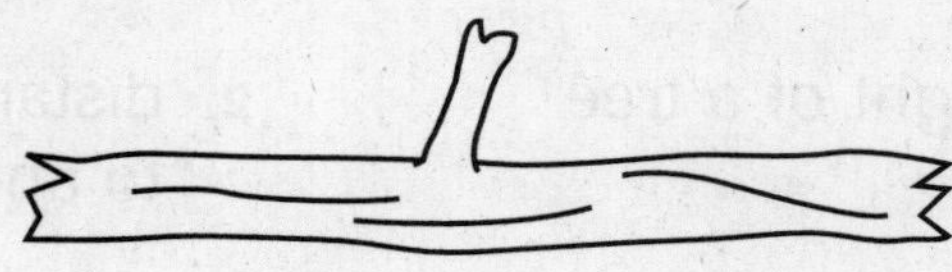

______________________ ______________________

______________________ ______________________

Choose the better estimate.

3. length of a shoe
20 cm or 20 mm
____

4. length of a paper clip
3 cm or 3 dm
____

5. width of your wrist
4 cm or 14 cm
____

6. width of a refrigerator
6 dm or 60 dm
____

7. width of notebook
20 cm or 4 mm
____

8. width of a calculator
3 cm or 1 dm
____

Compare. Write >, <, or = for each ◯.

9. 5 cm ◯ 5 dm
10. 6 mm ◯ 60 dm
11. 30 cm ◯ 3 dm
12. 15 dm ◯ 15 mm
13. 200 cm ◯ 20 dm
14. 50 cm ◯ 500 dm

Test Prep

15. Which is the best estimate of the length of a spoon?

A 16 cm
B 16 dm
C 6 mm
D 60 dm

16. Beth needs to measure the yarn. What is the length of the yarn to the nearest centimeter? Explain how you found your answer.

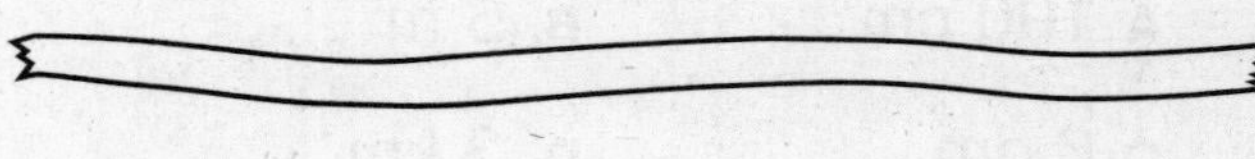

____

____

Use with text pages 382–383.

Name ______________________ Date __________

Practice 14.2

Meter and Kilometer

Choose the unit you would use to measure each. Write *m* or *km*.

1. height of a tree ________

2. distance from one city to another city ________

3. length of a rug ________

4. length of a gym ________

5. width of a wall ________

6. distance across two states ________

Choose the better estimate.

7. length of a basketball court 30 m or 30 km ________

8. width of a window 1 m or 1 km ________

9. height of a flagpole 6 m or 600 m ________

Complete.

10. 2 m = ______ cm

11. 5,000 m = ______ km

12. 30 dm = ______ m

Compare. Write >, <, or = for each ◯.

13. 400 m ◯ 1 km

14. 5 m ◯ 5,000 cm

15. 20 dm ◯ 2 m

Test Prep

16. Sal is measuring the length of a car. Which is the best estimate of the length of a car?

A 100 cm **B** 5 m

C 6 dm **D** 3 km

17. Oren measured 3 meters of wood. How many centimeters long is the wood? Explain how you found your answer.

____

____

____

Use with text pages 384–385.

Name ______________________ Date ____________

Practice 14.3

Metric Units of Capacity

Choose the better estimate for the capacity of each.

1.

2 L or 20 mL

____

2.

300 L or 300 mL

____

3.

8 L or 80 L

____

Choose the unit you would use to measure the capacity of each. Write *mL* or *L*.

4. a sink ______________

5. a container of eye drops ______________

6. a washing machine ______________

7. a toothpaste tube ______________

8. a measuring spoon ______________

9. a pitcher ______________

Complete.

10. 3 L = ________ mL

11. 6,000 mL = ________ L

12. 5 L = ________ mL

Compare. Write >, <, or = for each ◯.

13. 4,000 mL ◯ 4 L

14. 2 L ◯ 5,000 mL

15. 500 mL ◯ 1 L

Test Prep

16. Theo is using a pot to make soup. Which is the best estimate of the capacity of the pot?

A 50 L

B 5 mL

C 50 mL

D 5 L

17. A baker used 2 L of water for a batch of bread. How many mL of water did the baker use? Explain how you found your answer.

____

____

____

Use with text pages 386–388.

Name ______________________ Date ______________

Practice 14.4

Problem-Solving Strategy: Work Backward

Work backward to solve each problem. **Show your work.**

1. Will made his sign for water skiing lessons by cutting a board into 2 equal sections. Then he cut 9 centimeters off the one piece he wanted to use. This gave him a sign that was 41 centimeters long. How long was Will's original board?

____

2. Kate sailed her boat 7 kilometers to the city dock to buy supplies. Then she and a friend sailed 15 kilometers to a coral reef to snorkel. After that, she sailed home. She sailed 35 kilometers in all. How far does Kate live from the coral reef?

____

3. MJ caught 27 crabs in one of his crab pots and 32 crabs in his other crab pot. He threw some of the crabs back in the water because they were too small. He came home with 44 crabs. How many crabs did MJ throw back?

____

4. At the beach, Claudia bought a surfboard for $175 and two wetsuits. Each wetsuit was the same price. The three items together cost $335. How much did each wetsuit cost?

____

Use with text pages 390–392.

Name ______________________ Date ____________

Practice 14.5

Metric Units of Mass

Choose the unit you would use to measure the mass of each. Write *g* or *kg*.

1. a ruler ____________

2. a computer printer ____________

3. a computer disk ____________

4. a tomato ____________

5. an envelope ____________

6. a bicycle ____________

Choose the better estimate.

7. a book
1 g or 1 kg ____________

8. a peanut
1 g or 100 g ____________

9. a pair of boots
200 kg or 2 kg ____________

10. a scarf
60 g or 60 kg ____________

11. a car
800 g or 800 kg ____________

12. a bowling ball
70 g or 7 kg ____________

Complete.

13. 2,000 g = ______ kg

14. 6,000 g = ______ kg

15. 1 kg = ______ g

Compare. Write >, <, or = for each ◯.

16. 700 g ◯ 1 kg

17. 3 g ◯ 3,000 kg

18. 5 kg ◯ 5,000 g

19. Roberto measured the mass of a ring. Which is the best estimate of the mass of a ring?

A 4 g
B 4 kg
C 700 g
D 700 kg

20. Wanda measured the mass of a pumpkin. The pumpkin had a mass of 8 kg. How many grams of mass did the pumpkin have? Explain how you found your answer.

____

____

Use with text pages 394–396.

Name ______________________ Date ______________

Practice 15.1

Lines, Line Segments, Rays, and Angles

Write whether each figure is a *line, line segment,* or *ray.*

1. 

____

2. 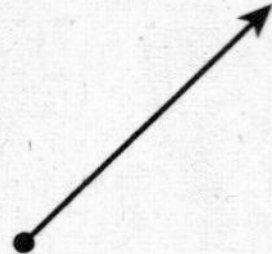

____

3. 

____

4. 

____

Tell whether each angle is a *right angle, less than a right angle,* or *greater than a right angle.*

5. 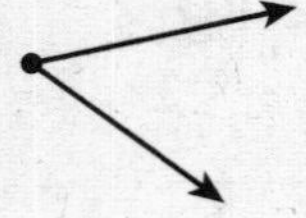

____

6. 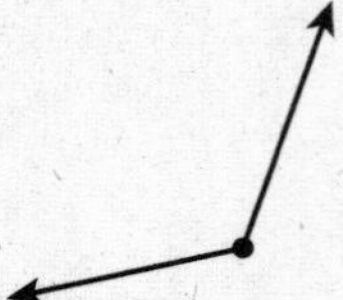

____

7. 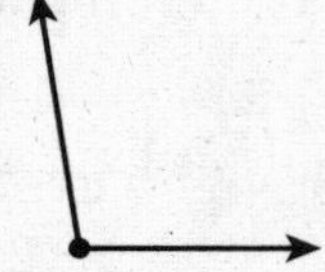

____

8. 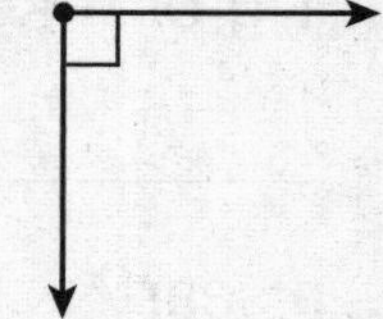

____

Tell whether each pair of lines is *parallel, intersecting,* or *perpendicular.*

9. 

____

10. 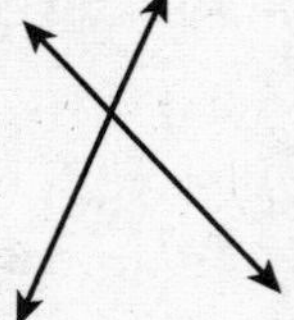

____

11. 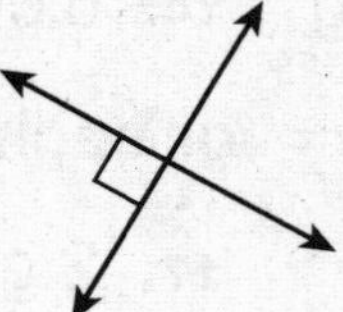

____

12. 

____

Test Prep

13. How many angles greater than 90° are shown in the figure below?

A 2 **C** 3

B 4 **D** 5

14. For the statement below, write *true* or *false*. Draw a picture to explain your answer. A line segment goes on without end.

____

Use with text pages 414–417.

Name ______________________ Date ____________

Practice 15.2

Classify Plane Figures

Tell whether each figure is a polygon. If it is, write its name.

1. 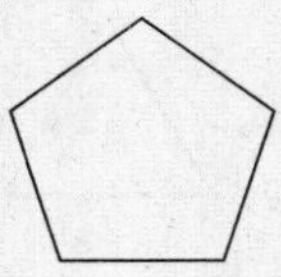

______

2. 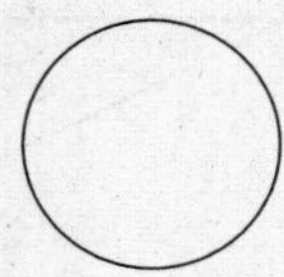

______

3. 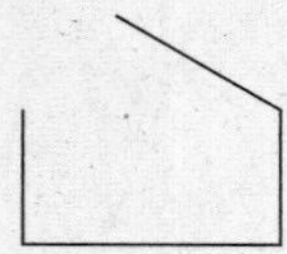

______

4. 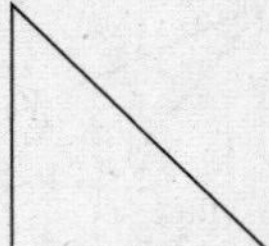

______

Use the plane figures at the right to answer Questions 5–7.

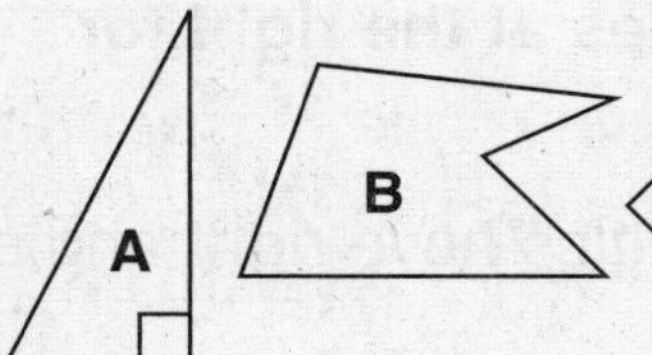

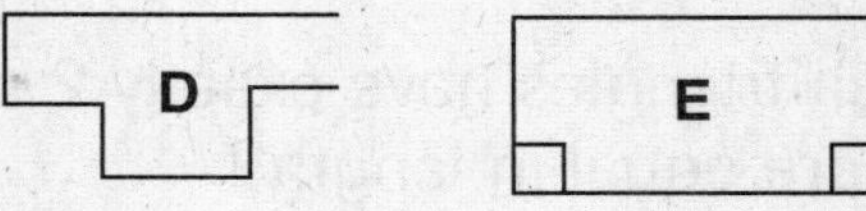

5. Which plane figures have right angles?

______

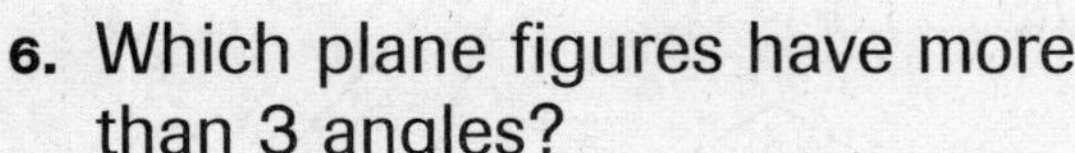

6. Which plane figures have more than 3 angles?

______

7. Which plane figures have more than 4 vertices?

______

Test Prep

8. Travis drew an irregular polygon. Which figure did he draw?

A 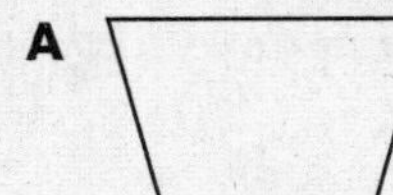

C 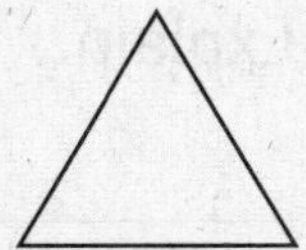

B 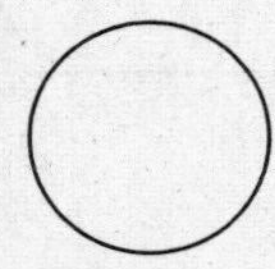

D 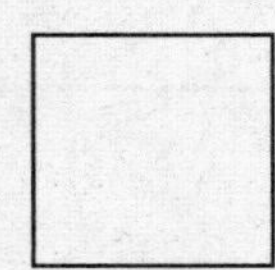

9. Flora drew the figure below. Is it a polygon? Explain why or why not.

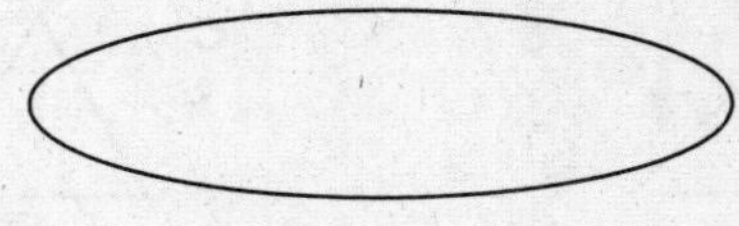

______

______

Use with text pages 418–421.

Name ______________________ Date ____________

Practice 15.3

Classify Triangles

Name the kind of triangle shown. Write *equilateral*, *isosceles*, *right*, or *scalene*.

1. 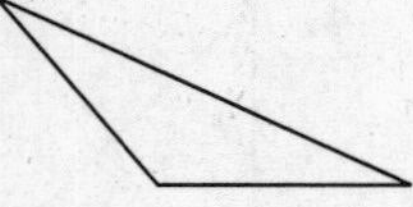

____

2. 

____

3. 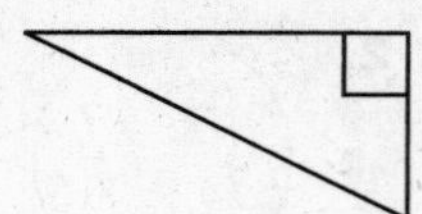

____

4. 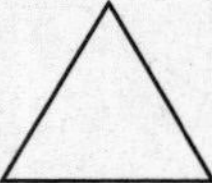

____

Use the triangles at the right for Problems 5–7.

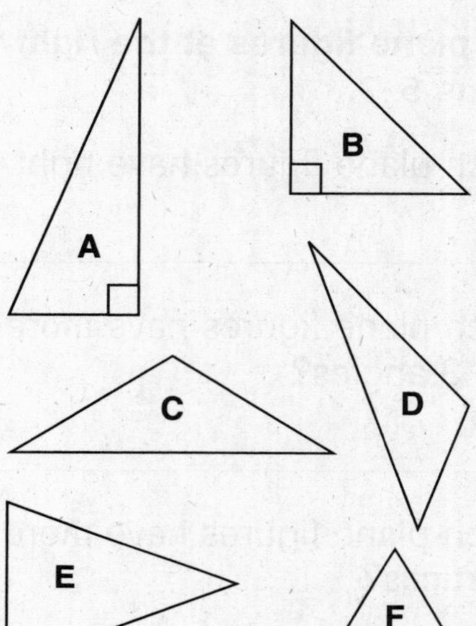

5. Which triangles have right angles?

____

6. Which triangles have exactly 2 sides that are equal in length?

____

7. Which triangles have each side a different length?

____

Test Prep

8. Ryan drew a scalene triangle. Which triangle did he draw?

A 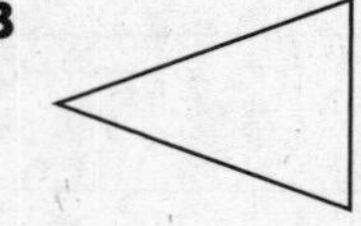

C 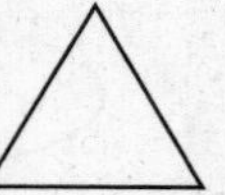

B

D 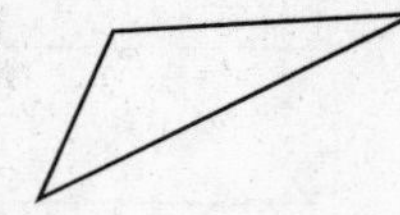

9. Hilda drew a triangle with sides that are 10 cm, 10 cm, and 12 cm long. What kind of triangle did she draw? Explain.

____

____

Use with text pages 422–423.

Name ______________________ Date ____________

Practice 15.4

Classify Quadrilaterals

Tell whether the figure is a quadrilateral. If it has a special name, write it.

1. 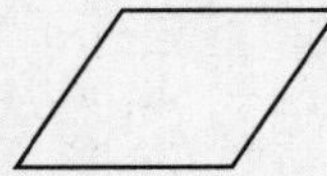 ____________

2. 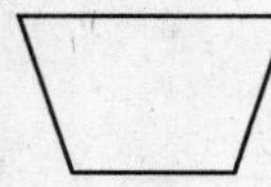 ____________

3.  ____________

4. 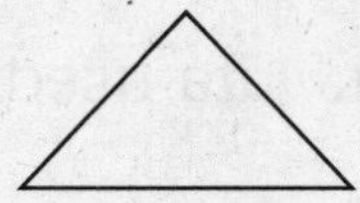 ____________

Write *true* or *false* for each. Draw a picture to explain your answer.

5. A parallelogram has exactly 1 pair of parallel sides.

____

6. A square has 4 equal sides.

____

Use the figure at the right for Problem 7.

7. Draw a diagonal from *B* to *E*. What 2 polygons are formed?

____

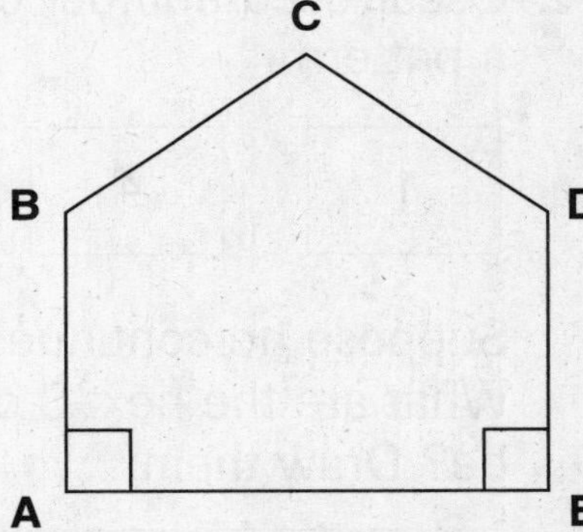

Test Prep

8. Molly drew a quadrilateral with opposite sides that are parallel. Which of the figures was NOT the figure Molly drew?

A 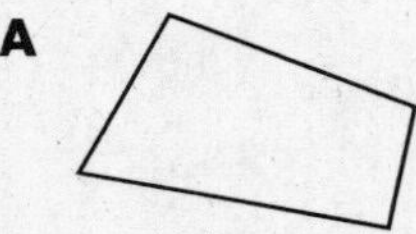

C 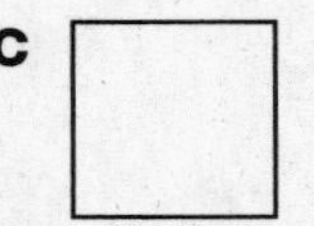

B 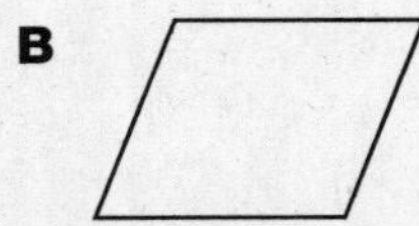

D 

9. Juan drew a quadrilateral. It had 4 equal sides and 4 right angles. What is the name of the quadrilateral that Juan drew?

____

Name ______________________________ Date ____________

Practice 15.5

Problem-Solving Strategy: Find a Pattern

Use a pattern to solve each problem.

Show your work.

1. Lita used shapes to make a pattern.

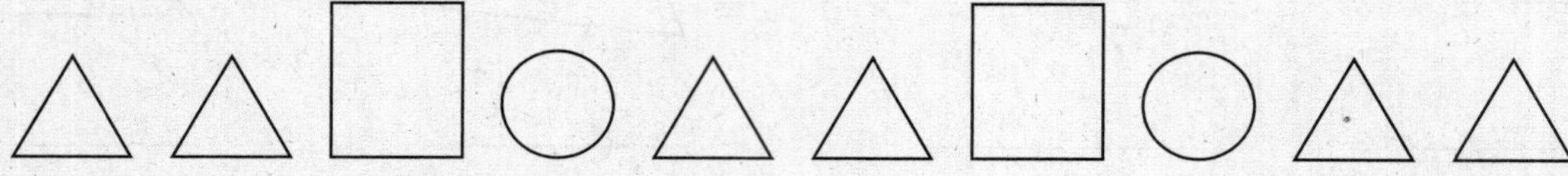

Suppose she continues her pattern. What are the next 3 shapes likely to be? Draw them.

2. Oscar used number cards to make a pattern.

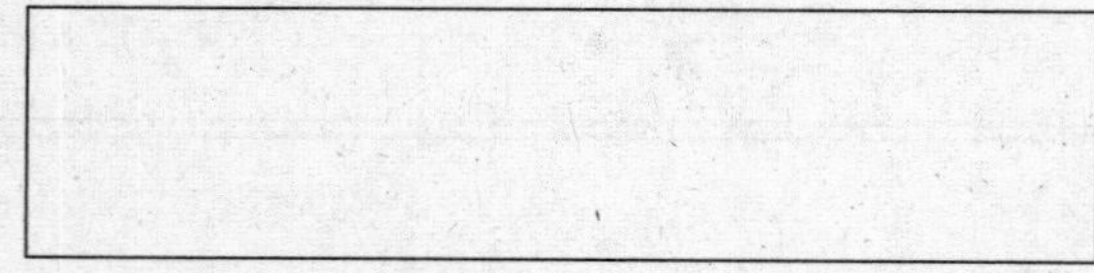

Suppose he continues his pattern. What are the next 3 cards likely to be? Draw them.

3. Sofi uses beads to make rings. She strings together these color beads: green, blue, red, red, green, blue, red, red, green, blue. If she continues her pattern, what colors will the next three beads be?

____

____

Use with text pages 428–430.

Name ______________________ Date ____________

Practice 15.6

Solid Figures

Name the solid figure that each object looks like.

1. 

____

2. 

____

3. 
____

4. 
____

Name the solid figures that make up each object.

5. 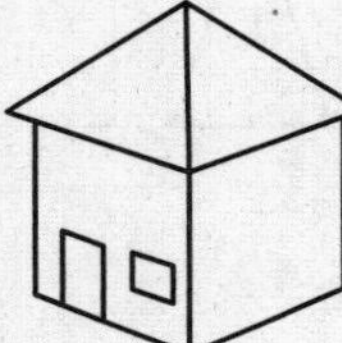
____
____

6. 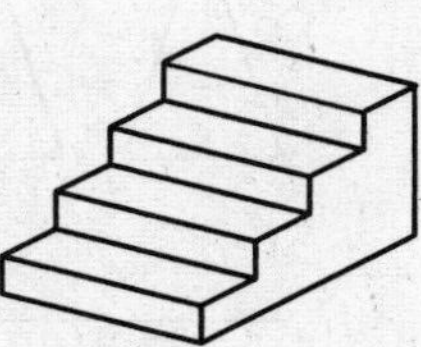
____
____

7. 
____
____

8. 
____
____

Test Prep

9. Marty drew a cylinder. Which figure below did Marty draw?

A 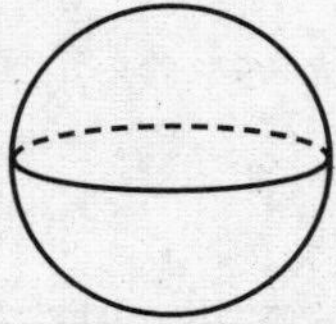

C 

B 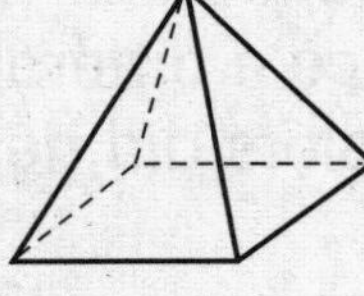

D 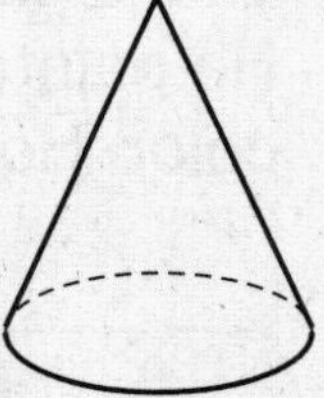

10. Devan is building with toy blocks. He wants to use some solid figures that roll. Which solid figures can roll?

____

____

Name ______________________ Date ____________

Practice 15.7

Explore Solid Figures

Connect the plane figures with line segments. Name the solid figure you drew.

1. 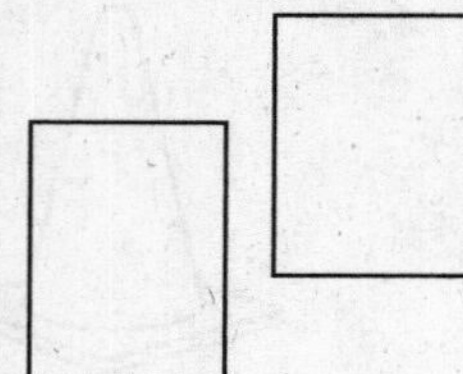

2. 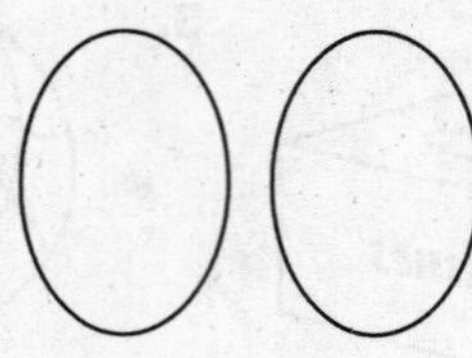

3. 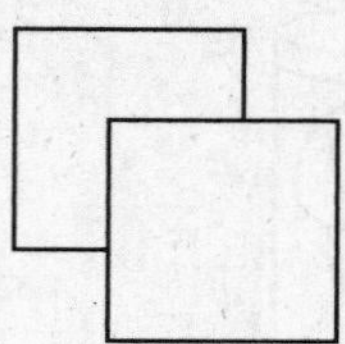

______________ ______________ ______________

Name the solid figures that have the faces shown.

4. 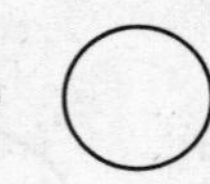

____

5. 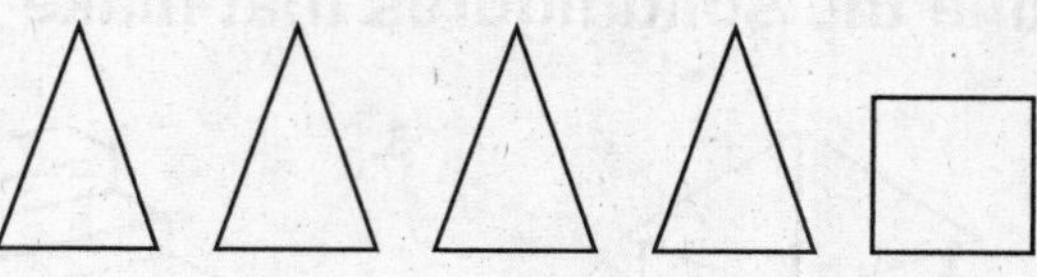

____

Write *true* or *false* for each. If false, write a statement that is true.

6. One face of a rectangular prism is a circle.

____

7. A cube has 8 faces.

____

Test Prep

8. Luann drew a solid figure. One of its faces is a square. Which solid did she draw?

A cone

B pyramid

C cylinder

D sphere

9. Tad is painting a rectangular prism. He painted each face a different color. How many colors did he use?

____

Name ______________________ Date ______________

Practice 16.1

Congruent Figures

Trace one of the two figures. Place the traced figure on top of the other figure. Are the figures in each pair congruent?

1. 

____

2. 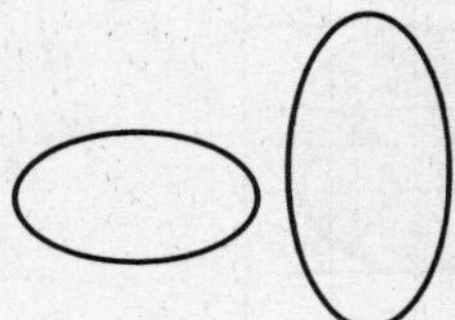

____

3. 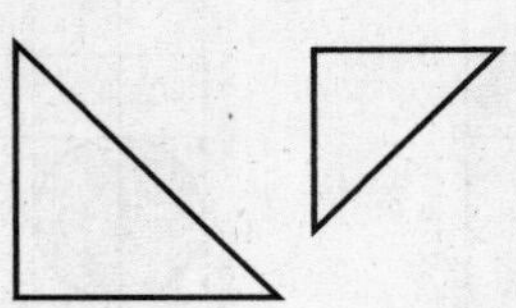

____

4. 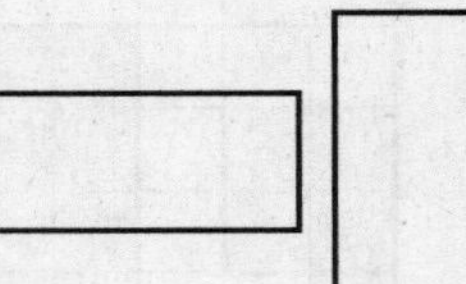

____

Trace the first figure. Place the traced figure on top of the other figures. Then choose the figure that is congruent to it. Write *a, b,* or *c*.

5. 

a 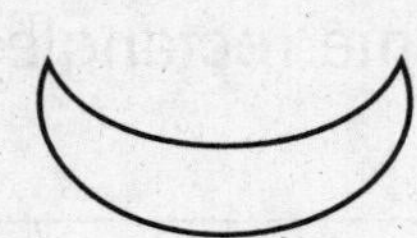

b 

c 

______

Test Prep

6. Which figure is congruent to the shaded figure?

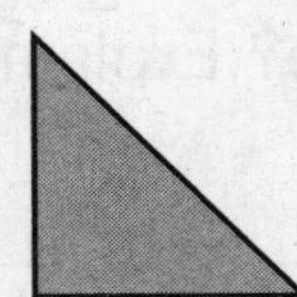

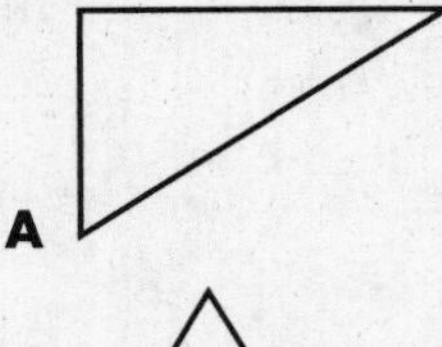

A

C

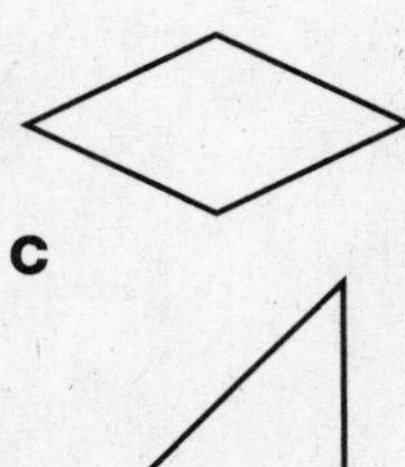

B

D

7. Barry drew a square. Ned drew a square. Is Barry's figure congruent to Ned's figure, for certain? Explain your answer.

____

____

____

Use with text pages 442–443.

Name ______________________ Date ____________

Practice 16.2

Similar Figures

Tell whether the two figures in each exercise are similar.

1. 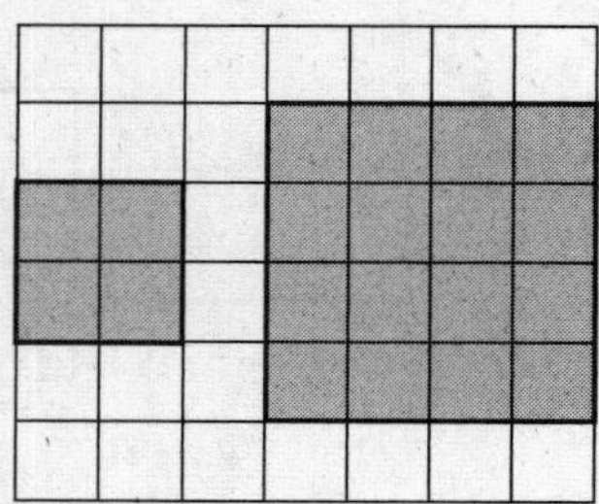

2. 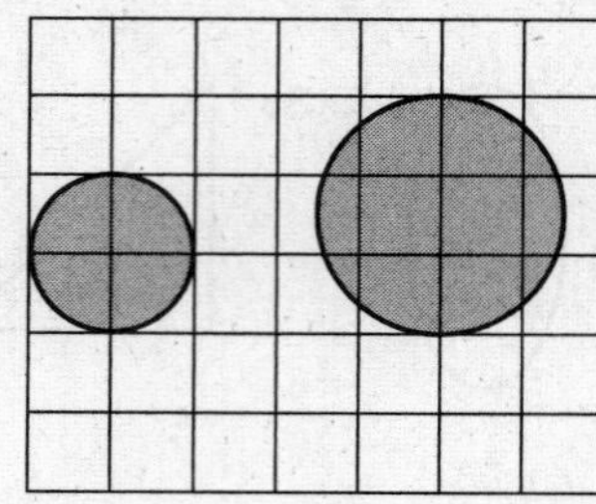

3. 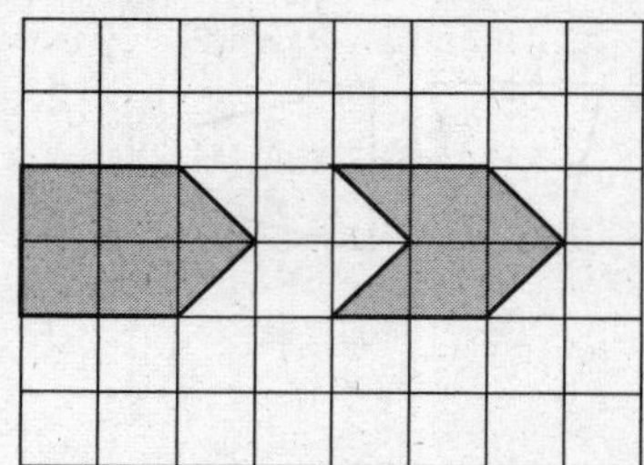

Write *true* or *false* for each sentence. Then write a sentence or draw an example to explain your answer.

4. All triangles are similar.

5. Some rectangles are similar.

6. All circles are similar.

7. No hexagons are congruent.

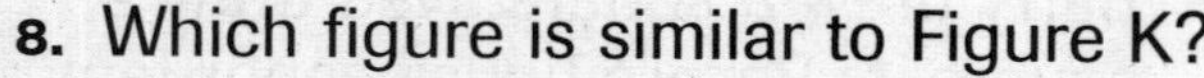

8. Which figure is similar to Figure K?

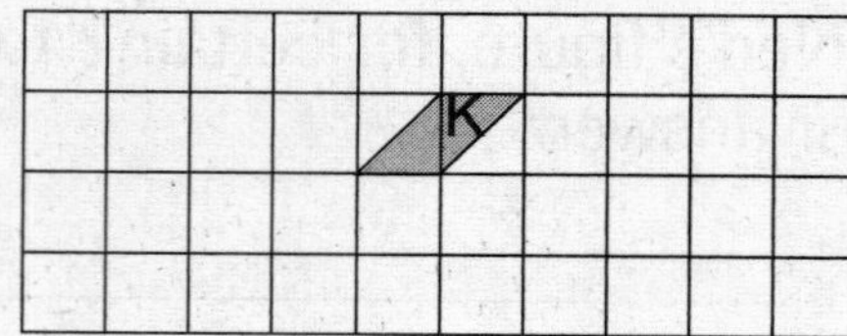

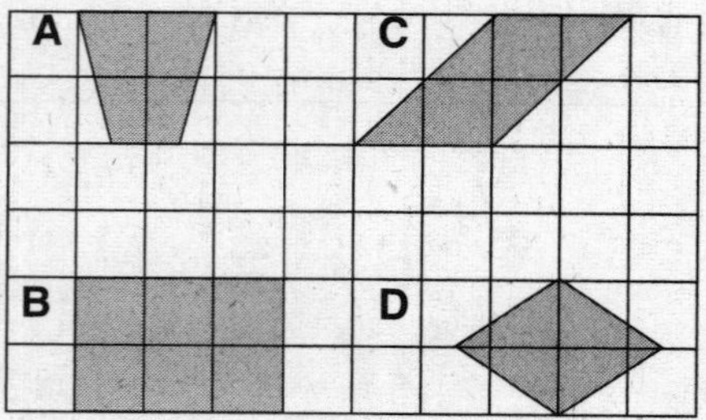

9. Lani drew a square. Trish drew a square. Is Lani's figure similar to Trish's figure? Explain your answer.

Use with text pages 444–446.

Name ______________________ Date ____________

Line of Symmetry

Trace and cut out each figure. Fold the figure and record how many lines of symmetry you find.

1. 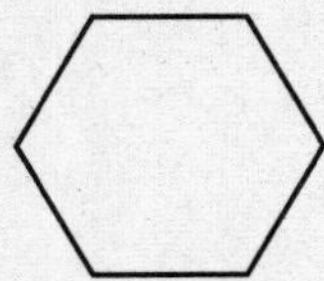

______

2. 

______

3. 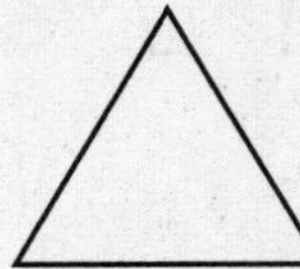

______

Tell whether each line appears to be a line of symmetry.

4. 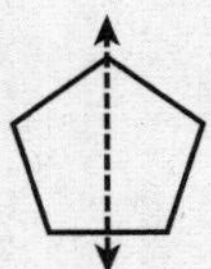

______

5. 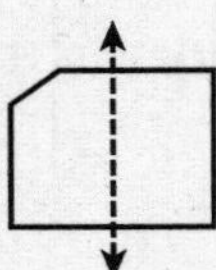

______

6. 

______

7. 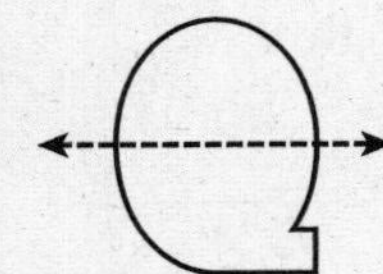

______

8. 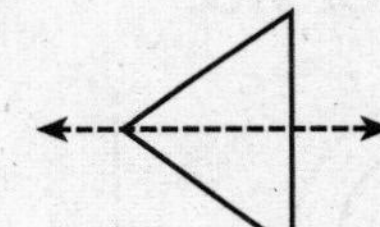

______

9. 

______

Test Prep

10. Which figure appears to have a line of symmetry?

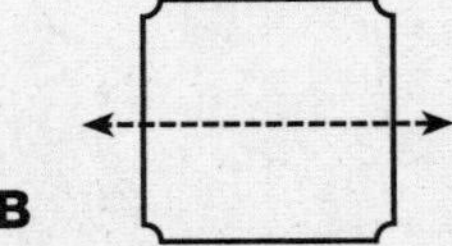

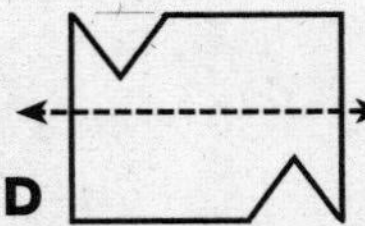

11. Draw an uppercase letter that has exactly 2 lines of symmetry. Then draw a letter that has just one line of symmetry.

Use with text pages 448–449.

Name ______________________ Date ____________

Practice 16.4

Transformations

Does the figure show a slide? Write *yes* or *no*.

1. 

____

2.  

____

Does the figure show a flip? Write *yes* or *no*.

3. 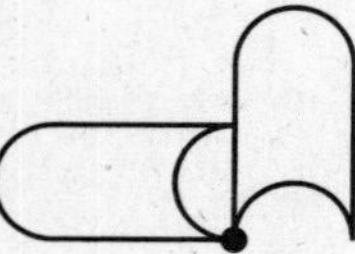

____

4. 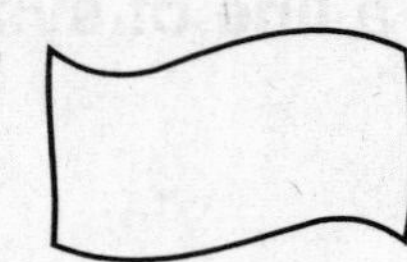 

____

Does the figure show a turn? Write *yes* or *no*.

5. 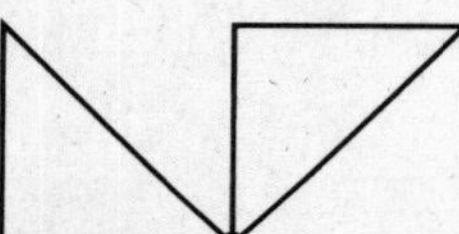

____

6. 

____

Test Prep

7. Look at the pattern below. In which position will the eighth arrow be?

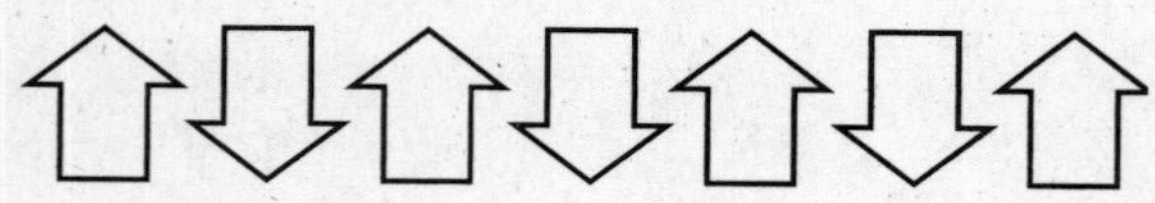

A 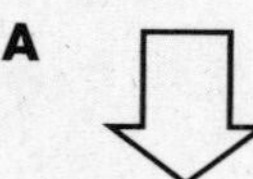

C 

B 

D  

8. When you turn a square a half turn, does it look the same as when you flip it? Explain.

____

____

Name ______________________ Date ____________

Practice 16.5

Problem-Solving Application: Visual Thinking

Use the tile design on the right for Problems 1–3.

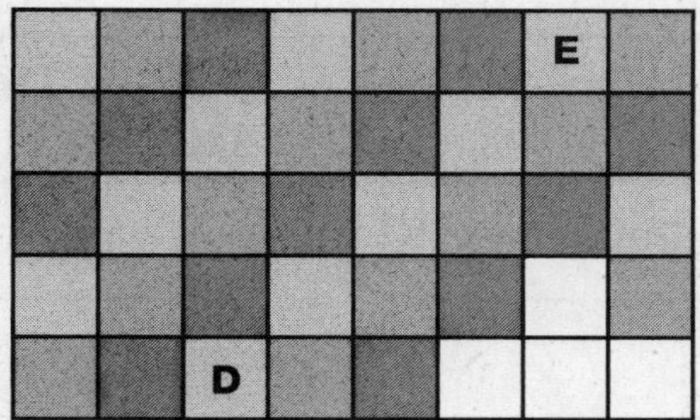

1. Miko made a pattern of tiles on her kitchen floor. Which set of tiles completes the pattern? Choose A, B, or C.

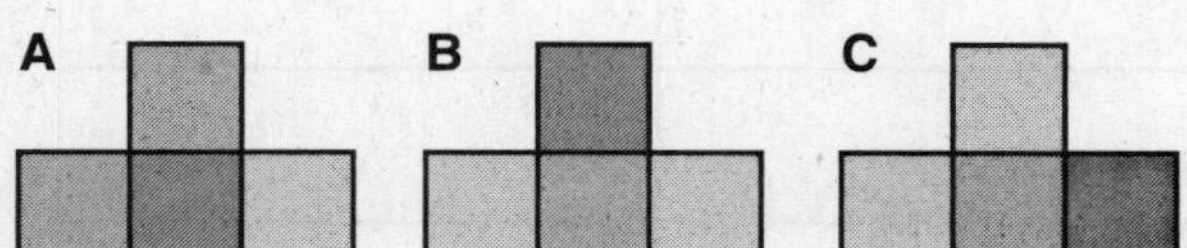

2. Miko is standing on Tile D. She is facing the missing tiles. She steps 2 tiles forward and turns left. Which color tile is on her left? Choose A, B, or C.

A  B 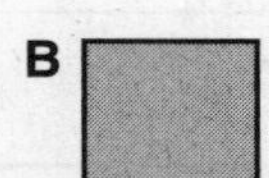 C 

3. Tony is standing on Tile E. He is facing the missing tiles. He steps 2 tiles forward. Which color tile is on his left? Choose A, B, or C.

A 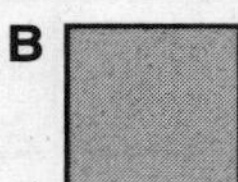 B  C

Test Prep

4. Look at the pattern below. Which is the missing piece of the pattern?

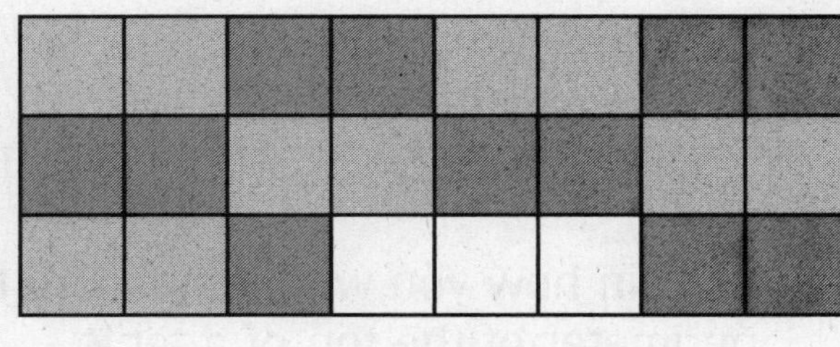

A

C

B

D 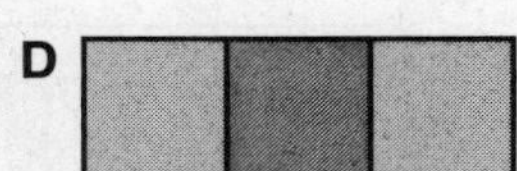

5. Ms. Kelly is planting tomato plants and lettuce plants. She wants 4 tomato plants for each lettuce plant. She will plant 6 rows of plants. Each row will have 1 lettuce plant. How many plants will she plant in all?

____

Use with text pages 454–456.

Name ____________________ Date ____________

Practice 17.1

Explore Perimeter

Complete the chart below. Trace a face of each object. Then estimate the perimeter of the face. Record your estimates. Then measure the perimeter using paper clips, toothpicks, and a ruler.

Object	Object Used to Measure	Estimate	Measurement
1. science book	paper clips		
	toothpick		
	ruler		
2. 3-ring binder	paper clips		
	toothpick		
	ruler		
3. magazine	paper clips		
	toothpick		
	ruler		

4. Which object has the greatest perimeter? The least perimeter?

____

Test Prep

5. Choose the best estimate of the perimeter of the top of a table.

A 2 inches **C** 90 inches

B 1,000 inches **D** 17,000 inches

6. Explain how you would measure the perimeter of the top of a table.

____

____

Use with text pages 462–463.

Name ______________________ Date ____________

Practice 17.2

Find Perimeter

Find the perimeter of each figure.

1.

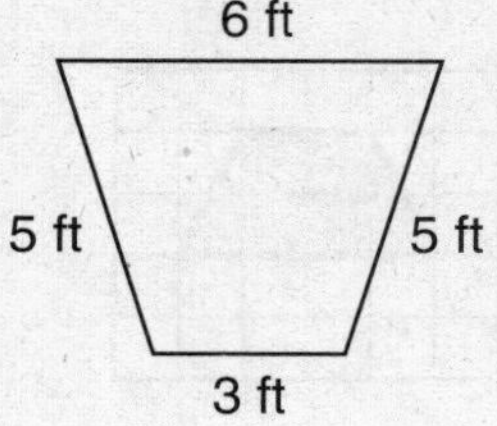

2.

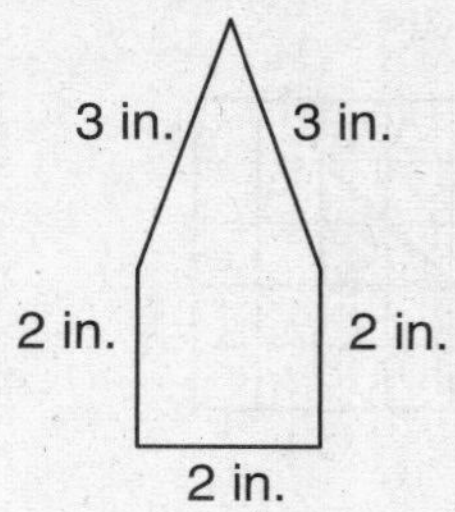

3.

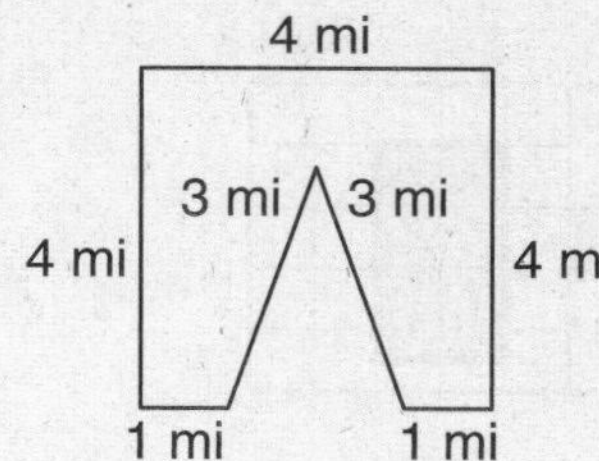

4.

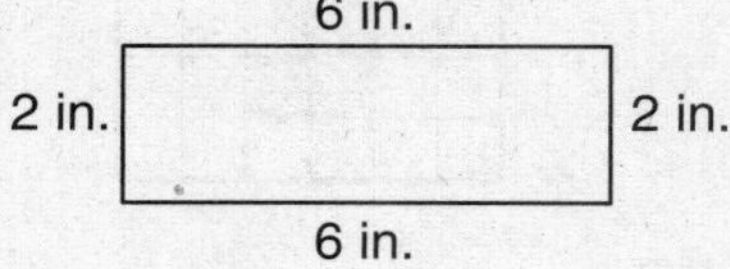

5.

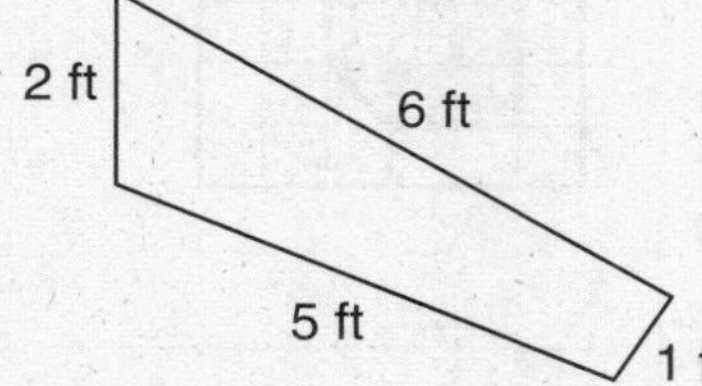

6.

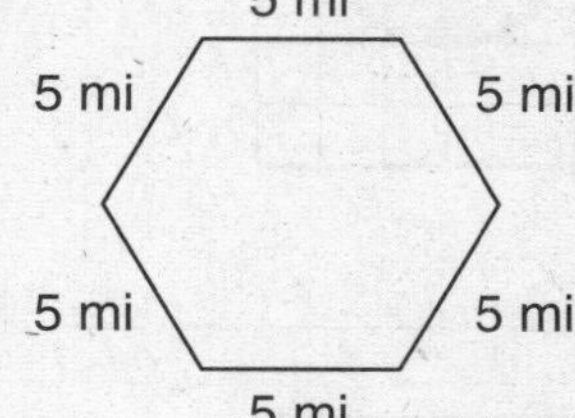

Measure the sides of each figure with a centimeter ruler. Then find the perimeter.

7.

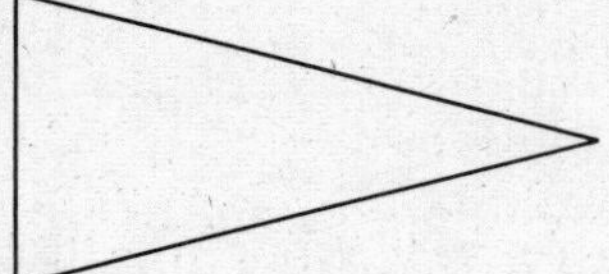

8.

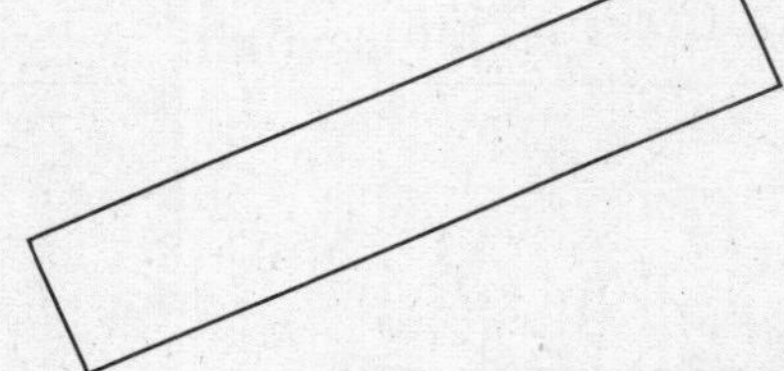

Test Prep

9. The perimeter of a triangle is 26 centimeters. The length of one side is 9 centimeters. The length of another side is 7 centimeters. What is the length of the third side?

A 10 cm **C** 11 cm

B 12 cm **D** 13 cm

10. The length of each side of a square is 8 inches. Explain how to find the perimeter of the square. What is the perimeter?

Name ______________________ Date ______________

Explore Area

Estimate the area of each figure. Each ☐ = 1 square unit.

1.

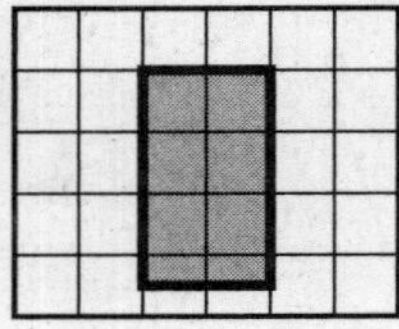

____

2.

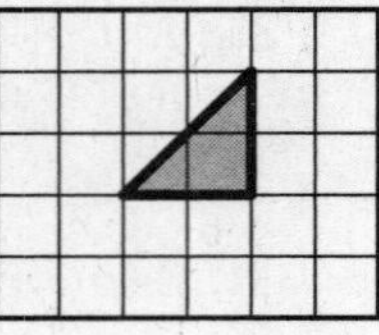

____

3.

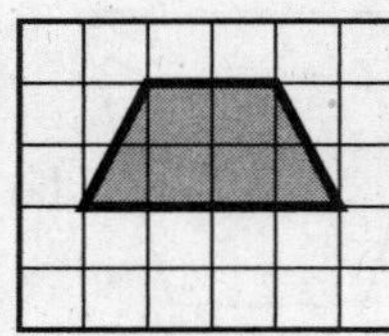

____

4.

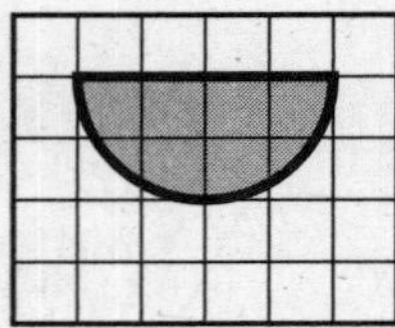

____

5.

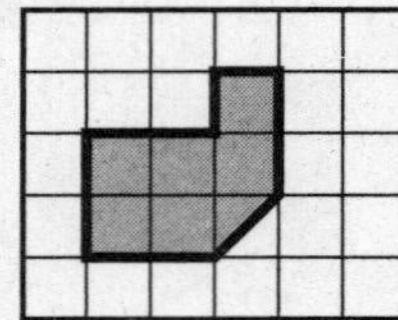

____

6.

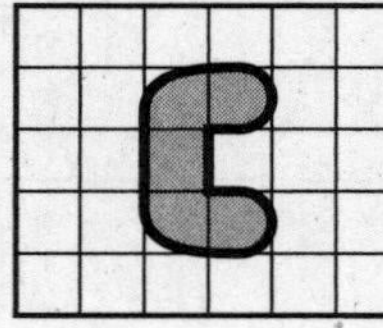

____

7.

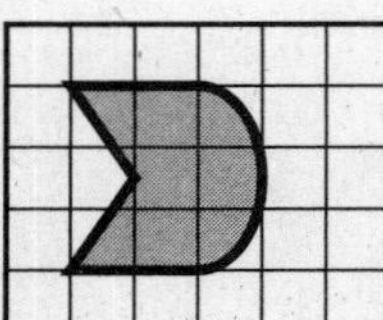

____

8.

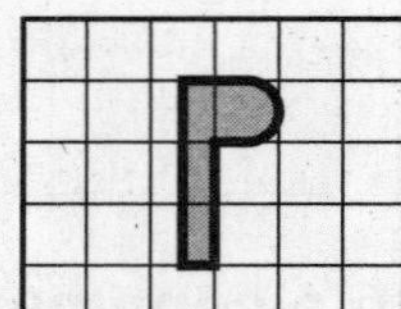

____

9.

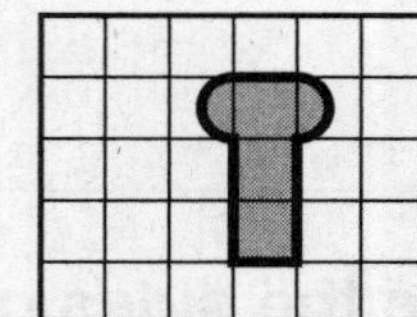

____

Test Prep

10. Choose the figure with an area of about 2 square units.

A

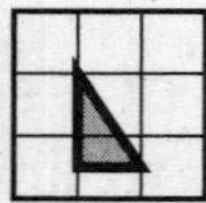

C

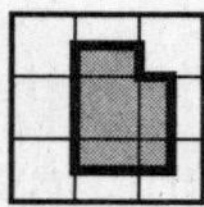

B

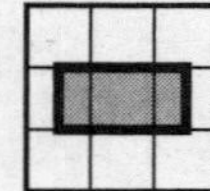

D

11. Look at exercises 1 and 4. Is it easier to estimate the area of a rectangle or a semi-circle? Explain.

____

____

____

____

Use with text pages 468–469.

Name ______________________ Date ____________

Practice 17.4

Find Area

Find the area of each figure. Label your answer in square units. Each □ or ⁚⁚ = 1 square unit.

1. 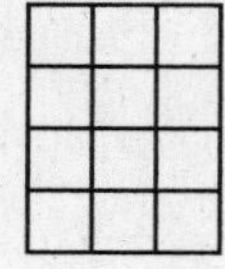

____

2. 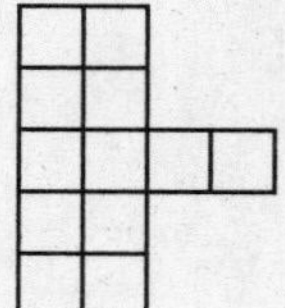

____

3. 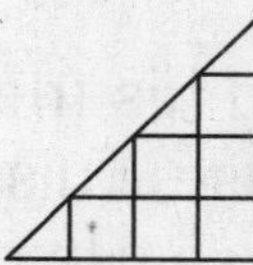

____

4. 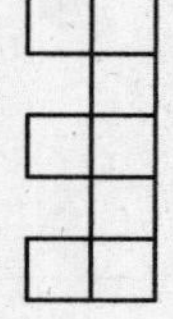

____

5. 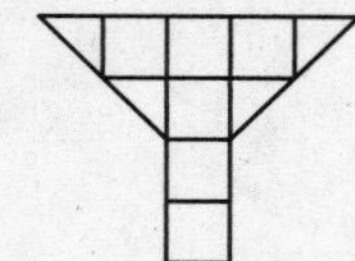

____

6. 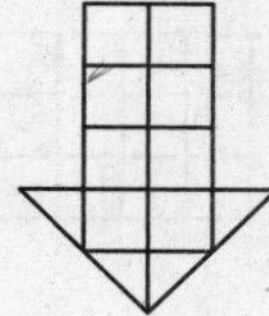

____

7.

____

8. 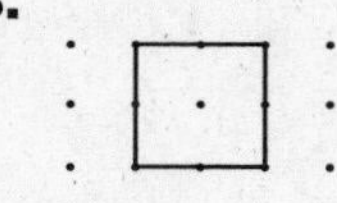

____

9. 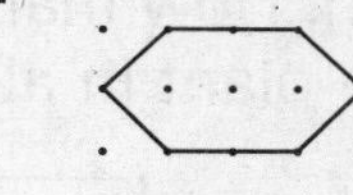

____

Test Prep

10. Choose the area of the figure.

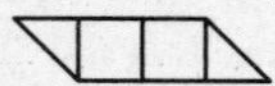

A 2 square units

B 3 square units

C $2\frac{1}{2}$ square units

D 4 square units

11. Draw a figure on grid paper with an area of 8 square units.

Name ______________________ Date ____________

Practice 17.5

Problem-Solving Application: Use Measurement

Use the diagrams to solve each problem.

Show your work.

1. Luis and his friends have a clubhouse. Luis made a table for the clubhouse. He covered the tabletop with square tiles. How many tiles did Luis use? What is the area of the tabletop in square units?

3 ft

9 ft

____

2. Cassie is planting two flowers in every square foot of the clubhouse garden. How many flowers will Cassie plant in all?

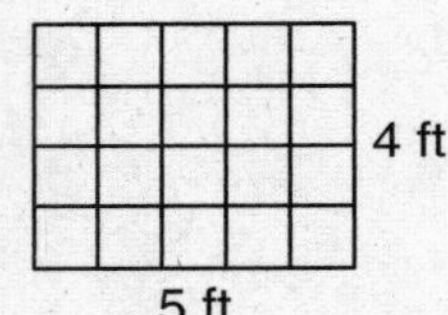

____

3. Isabel built a fence around the clubhouse. She didn't build any fence in front of the doors. There are 2 doors and each is 2 feet wide. How many feet of fence did Isabel build?

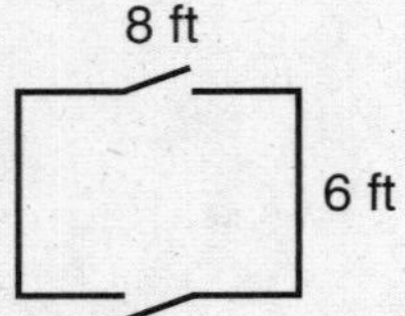

____

Use with text pages 474–475.

Name ______________________ Date ____________

Practice 17.6

Explore Volume

Estimate the volume of each figure. Then build it with cubes. Write the estimate and the number of cubes you used.

1.

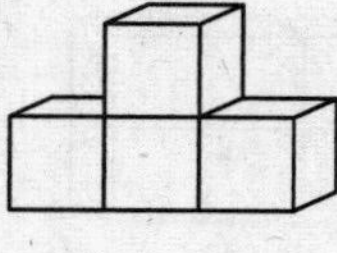

____

____

2.

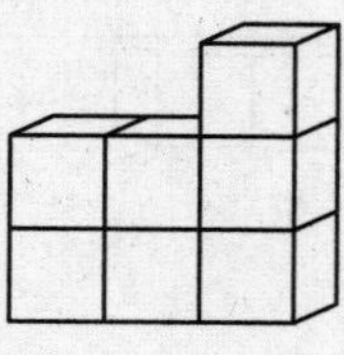

____

____

3.

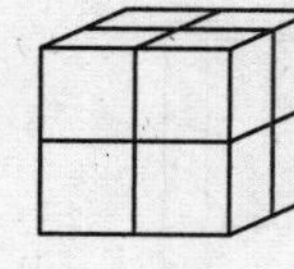

____

____

4.

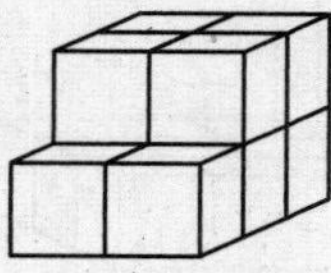

____

____

5.

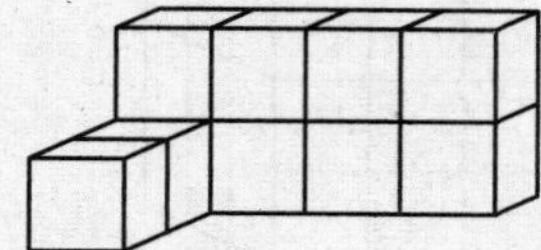

____

____

6.

____

____

7.

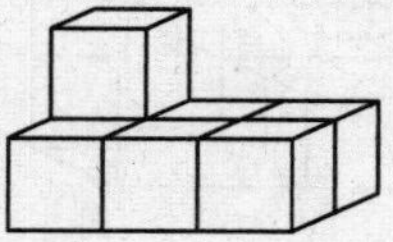

____

____

8.

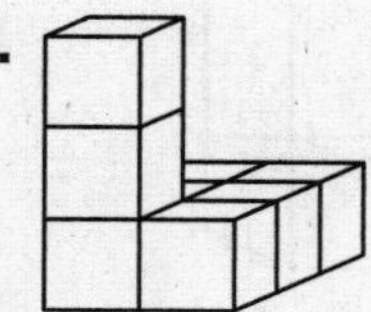

____

____

9.

____

____

Test Prep

10. Choose the word that means the number of unit cubes that make up a solid figure.

A perimeter **C** area

B volume **D** length

11. Sketch a solid figure with a volume of 11 unit cubes.

____

____

____

Use with text pages 476–477.

Name ______________________ Date ____________

Practice 17.7

Find Volume

Find the volume of each figure. Each
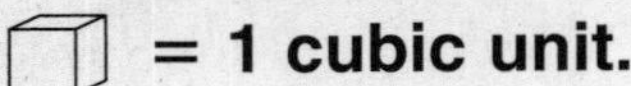
= 1 cubic unit.

1.
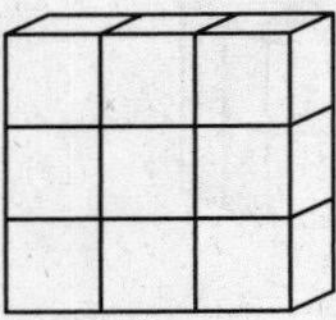
____

2.
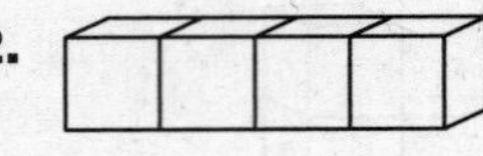
____

3.
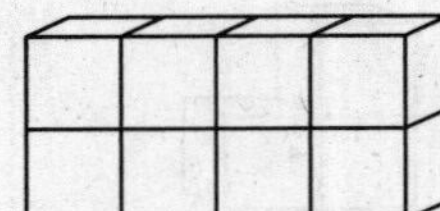
____

4.
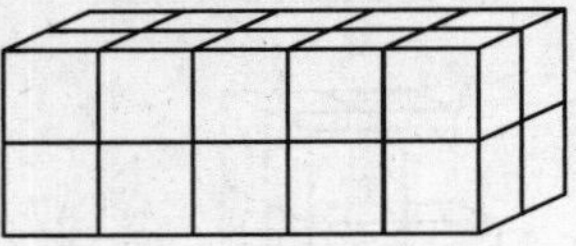
____

5.
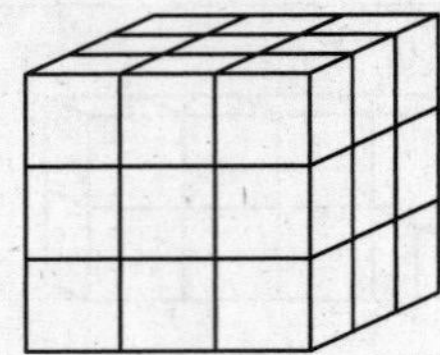
____

6.
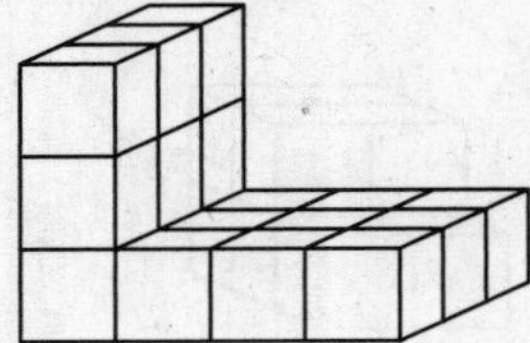
____

Estimate the volume of each container in unit cubes.

7.
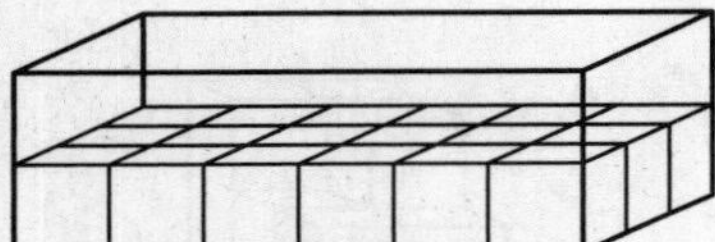
____

8.
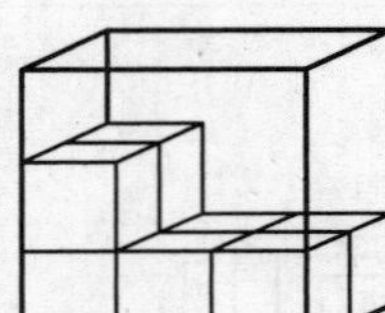
____

9.
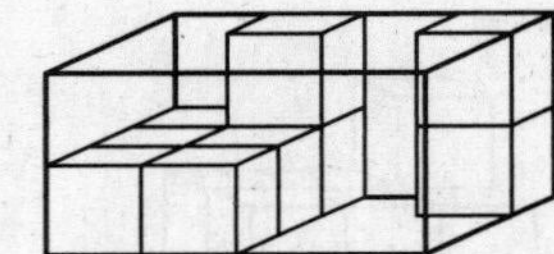
____

10. Choose the volume of the figure.

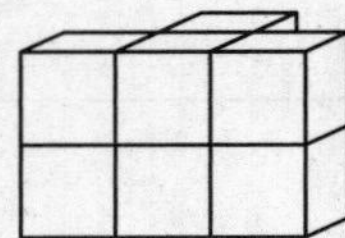

A 5 cubic units
C 6 cubic units
B 7 cubic units
D 8 cubic units

11. Describe two different ways to find the volume of the figure in Problem 10.

____

____

Use with text pages 478–480.

Name ______________________________ Date ______________

Practice 18.1

Fractions and Regions

Write a fraction for the part that is shaded. Then write a fraction for the part that is not shaded.

1. 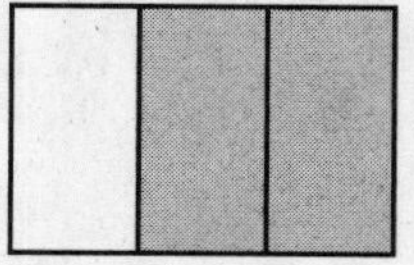

Shaded: ______

Not Shaded: ______

2. 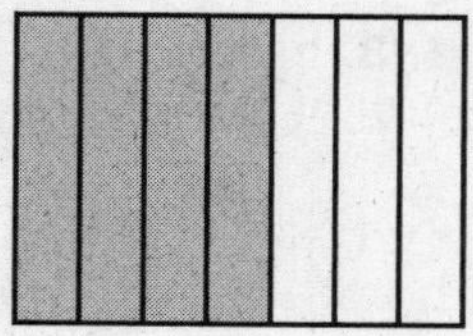

Shaded: ______

Not Shaded: ______

3. 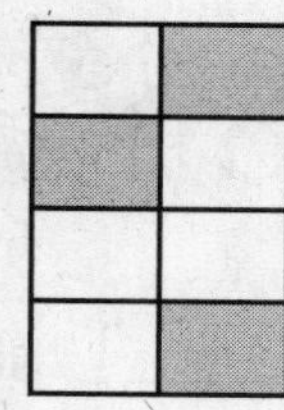

Shaded: ______

Not Shaded: ______

4. 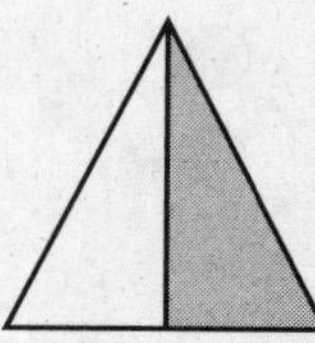

Shaded: ______

Not Shaded: ______

5. 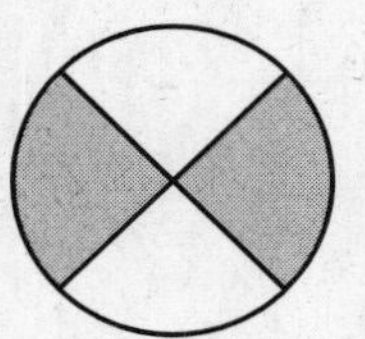

Shaded: ______

Not Shaded: ______

6. 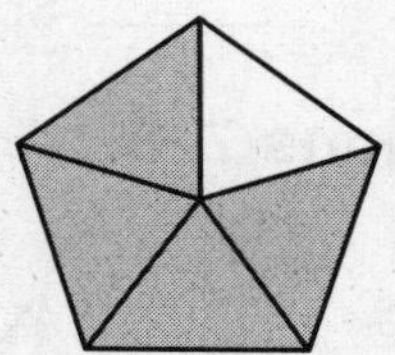

Shaded: ______

Not Shaded: ______

7. 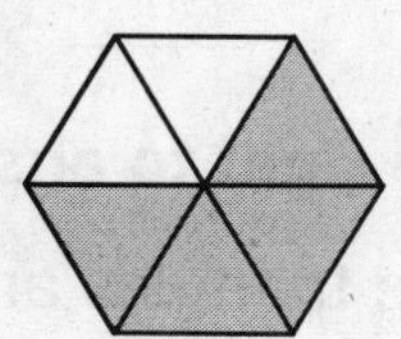

Shaded: ______

Not Shaded: ______

8. 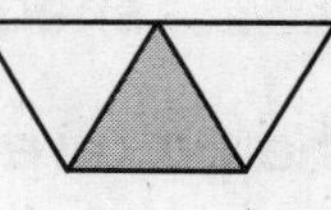

Shaded: ______

Not Shaded: ______

Draw a picture to show each fraction.

9. $\frac{3}{4}$

10. $\frac{8}{10}$

11. $\frac{2}{7}$

12. $\frac{1}{2}$

13. $\frac{4}{5}$

14. $\frac{5}{6}$

Test Prep

15. Which of these figures has $\frac{3}{4}$ shaded?

A 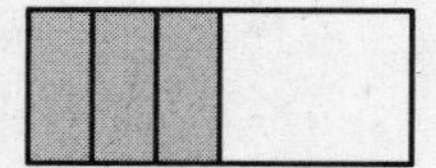

C 

B

D 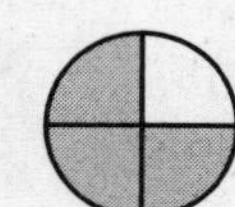

16. Isabel drew a figure. The figure had 6 equal parts. She shaded $\frac{4}{6}$ of the figure. Draw a figure that has $\frac{4}{6}$ shaded.

Use with text pages 498–499.

Name ______________________ Date ____________

Practice 18.2

Fractions and Groups

Write a fraction to name the part of each group that is shaded.

1. 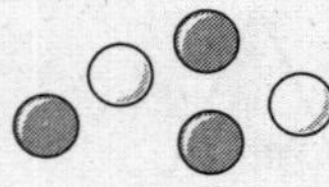

_____ shaded

2. 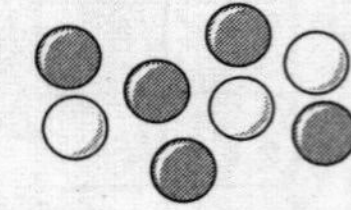

_____ shaded

3. 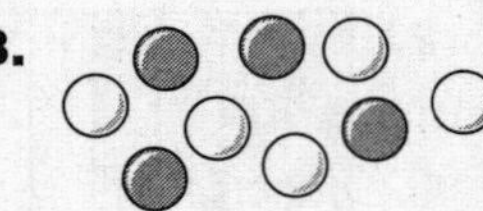

_____ shaded

4. 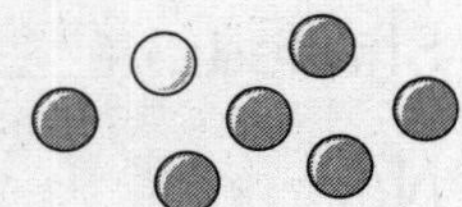

_____ shaded

5. 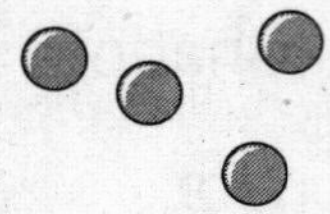

_____ shaded

6. 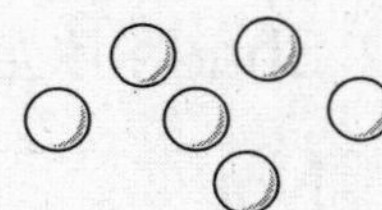

_____ shaded

Use the picture on the right to answer Questions 7–8.

7. What fraction of the triangles are striped?

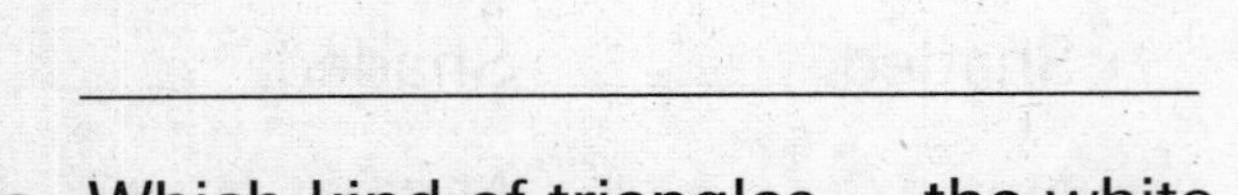

8. Which kind of triangles – the white, the shaded, or the striped – are $\frac{1}{8}$ of the group?

____

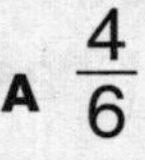

Test Prep

9. Marcus has 10 beads. He painted 4 of the beads blue. He painted 6 of the beads yellow. What fraction of the beads did Marcus paint yellow?

   A $\frac{4}{6}$

   B $\frac{6}{10}$

   C $\frac{4}{10}$

   D $\frac{6}{4}$

10. Lorraine bought 5 peppers. One of the peppers is red. What fraction of the peppers are not red?

____

Use with text pages 500–501.

Name ______________________ Date ____________

Practice 18.3

Fractional Parts of a Group

Use counters to find each answer.

1. $\frac{1}{3}$ of 9

______

2. $\frac{1}{6}$ of 12

______

3. $\frac{3}{4}$ of 8

______

4. $\frac{2}{5}$ of 15

______

5. $\frac{3}{4}$ of 16

______

6. $\frac{2}{2}$ of 14

______

7. $\frac{3}{5}$ of 25

______

8. $\frac{2}{3}$ of 6

______

9. $\frac{3}{6}$ of 18

______

Test Prep

10. Lourdes has 20 beads. One fourth of the beads are green. How many green beads does Lourdes have?

A 1 C 4

B 5 D 14

11. David planted 18 plants. Five sixths of the plants are tomato plants. How many of the plants are tomato plants?

______

Use with text pages 502–504.

Name ______________________ Date ____________

Practice 18.4

Problem-Solving Application: Multistep Problems

Solve.

Show your work.

1. The sewing club made a quilt to celebrate Earth Day. The quilt has 6 rows of 5 equal squares. Lydia made $\frac{1}{3}$ of the quilt squares. How many quilt squares did Lydia make?

   ____

2. Donny had 5 packs each of red, white, blue, and black buttons in his sewing room. Each pack had 2 buttons. He used $\frac{1}{8}$ of the buttons to make his costume for the school play. How many buttons did he use?

   ____

3. Valerie bought 24 yards of calico cloth. She used $\frac{1}{4}$ of the cloth to make curtains. Then she used $\frac{1}{2}$ of the remaining cloth to make pillow covers. How many yards of cloth did she have left over?

   ____

4. Roger sewed 12 sock puppets for the craft fair. He sold $\frac{3}{4}$ of the puppets at the fair. He kept one of the remaining puppets for himself and gave the rest to his niece. How many puppets did Roger give to his niece?

   ____

Use with text pages 506–507.

Name ______________________ Date ______________

Practice 18.5

Model Equivalent Fractions

Write *equivalent* or *not equivalent* to describe the fractions in each pair.

1.

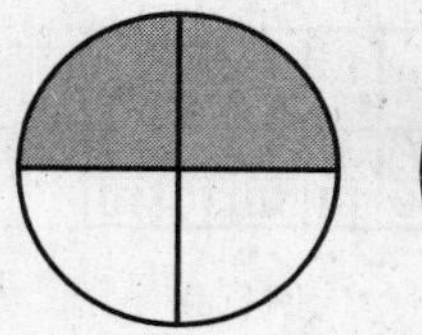 

____

2.

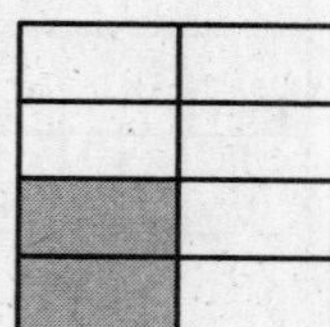 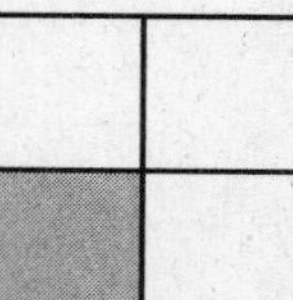

____

3.

____

4.

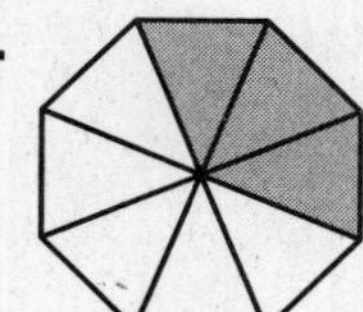 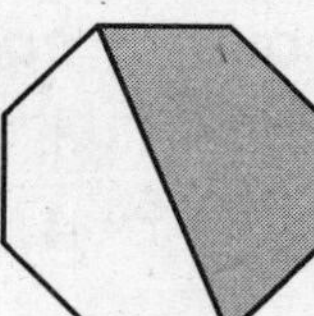

____

Use the circles to complete the equivalent fractions.

5.

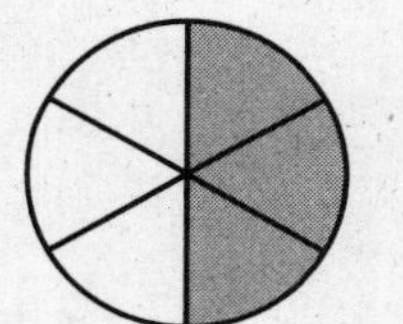

$\frac{3}{6} = \frac{■}{2}$

6.

 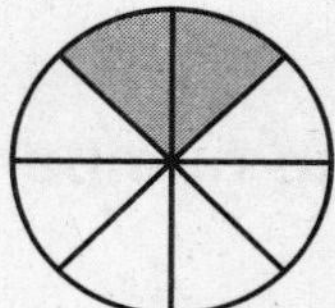

$\frac{1}{4} = \frac{■}{8}$

Test Prep

7. Mr. Haber bought 12 eggs. He used 4 of the eggs to make a cake. What is an equivalent fraction for the part of the eggs Mr. Haber used to make a cake?

A $\frac{3}{6}$

B $\frac{1}{3}$

C $\frac{3}{12}$

D $\frac{6}{12}$

8. Angie folded a circle into 8 equal parts. She colored all but 6 parts red. Write two equivalent fractions for the part of the circle that is not red.

____

Name ______________________ Date ____________

Practice 18.6

Find Equivalent Fractions

Name the equivalent fractions shown.

1.

1 whole			
$\frac{1}{2}$			
$\frac{1}{8}$	$\frac{1}{8}$	$\frac{1}{8}$	$\frac{1}{8}$

$\frac{1}{2} = \frac{■}{8}$

2.

1 whole			
$\frac{1}{3}$		$\frac{1}{3}$	
$\frac{1}{6}$	$\frac{1}{6}$	$\frac{1}{6}$	$\frac{1}{6}$

$\frac{2}{3} = \frac{■}{6}$

3.

1 whole							
$\frac{1}{5}$		$\frac{1}{5}$		$\frac{1}{5}$		$\frac{1}{5}$	
$\frac{1}{10}$	$\frac{1}{10}$	$\frac{1}{10}$	$\frac{1}{10}$	$\frac{1}{10}$	$\frac{1}{10}$	$\frac{1}{10}$	$\frac{1}{10}$

$\frac{4}{5} = \frac{■}{10}$

Draw fraction strips to compare the fractions. Write *equivalent* or *not equivalent*.

4. $\frac{1}{2}$ and $\frac{3}{6}$ ____________

5. $\frac{1}{4}$ and $\frac{3}{8}$ ____________

6. $\frac{1}{3}$ and $\frac{1}{8}$ ____________

7. $\frac{1}{3}$ and $\frac{2}{6}$ ____________

Find each missing number to make equivalent fractions.

8. $\frac{1}{4} = \frac{2}{8} = \frac{3}{12} = \frac{4}{16} = \frac{■}{20} = \frac{■}{24}$

9. $\frac{2}{3} = \frac{4}{6} = \frac{6}{9} = \frac{8}{12} = \frac{■}{15} = \frac{■}{18}$

Test Prep

10. Mrs. Cole cut a pie into 8 equal pieces. She served $\frac{1}{4}$ of the pie. How many pieces of the pie did Mrs. Cole serve?

A 1 **C** 2

B 4 **D** 8

11. Kathy ran $\frac{3}{4}$ mile. Lorraine ran $\frac{6}{8}$ mile. Did they run the same distance? Explain.

____

____

Use with text pages 510–511.

Name ______________________ Date ______________

Practice 18.7

Mixed Numbers

Write an improper fraction and a mixed number for the shaded parts.

1. 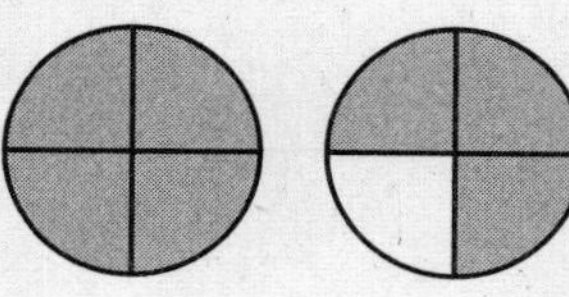
______

2. 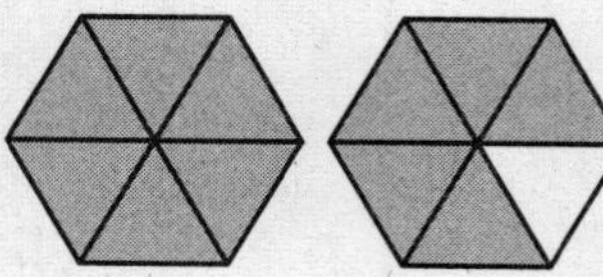
______

3. 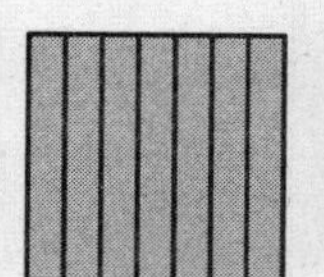 
______

Use the number line to help you write the mixed number.

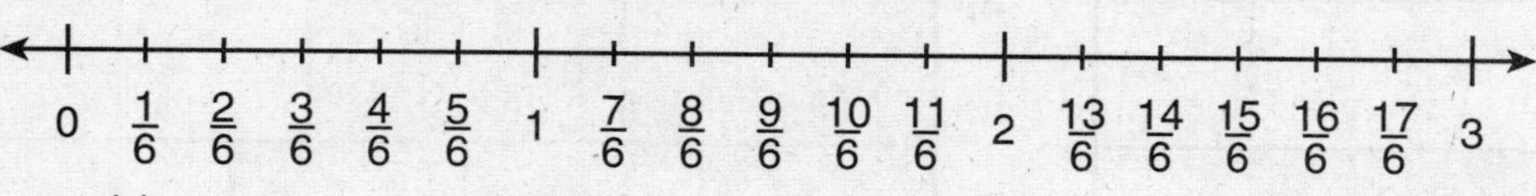

4. $\frac{11}{6}$ 5. $\frac{14}{6}$ 6. $\frac{7}{6}$ 7. $\frac{9}{6}$ 8. $\frac{13}{6}$

Draw a picture to show each improper fraction. Then write a whole number or a mixed number.

9. $\frac{6}{4}$ 10. $\frac{10}{6}$ 11. $\frac{12}{5}$ 12. $\frac{4}{2}$ 13. $\frac{7}{3}$

______ ______ ______ ______ ______

Find each missing number.

14. $\frac{5}{4} = \blacksquare\frac{1}{4}$ 15. $\frac{13}{5} = 2\frac{\blacksquare}{5}$ 16. $3\frac{1}{2} = \frac{\blacksquare}{2}$ 17. $\frac{\blacksquare}{6} = 1\frac{5}{6}$

Test Prep

18. Lena used 7 half-sheets of newspaper to make a ball. What mixed number shows the number of sheets of newspaper she used?

A $\frac{1}{2}$ C $3\frac{1}{2}$

B $4\frac{1}{2}$ D $7\frac{1}{2}$

19. Toby cut two pies into eighths. He served 11 pieces of pie. Write a mixed number to show the amount of pie that Toby served.

____

Use with text pages 512–514.

Name ____________________ Date ____________

Practice 19.1

Compare Fractions

Compare the fractions. Write < or > for each ◯.

1.

$\frac{1}{3}$ ◯ $\frac{2}{3}$

2. 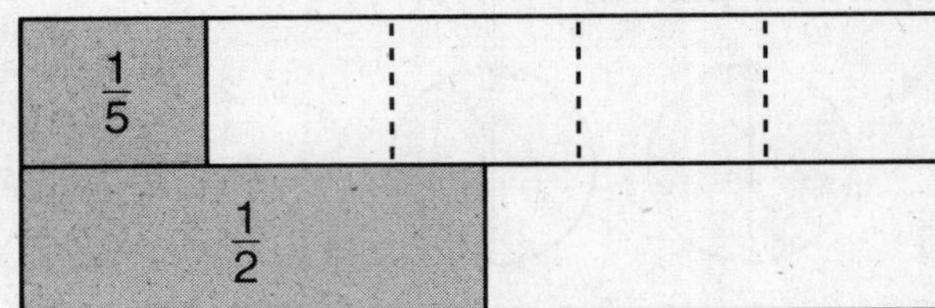

$\frac{1}{5}$ ◯ $\frac{1}{2}$

3. 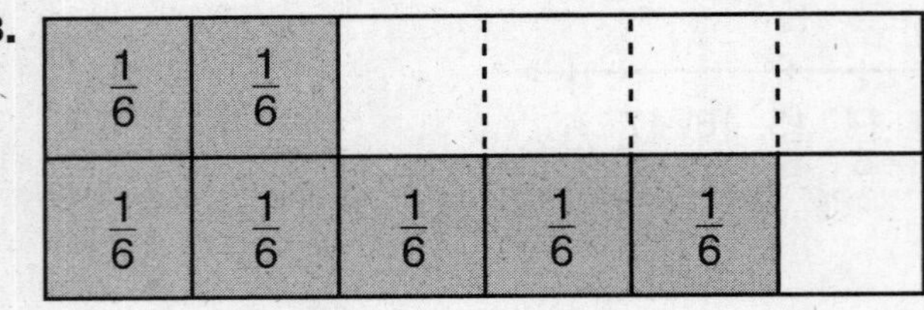

$\frac{2}{6}$ ◯ $\frac{5}{6}$

4. 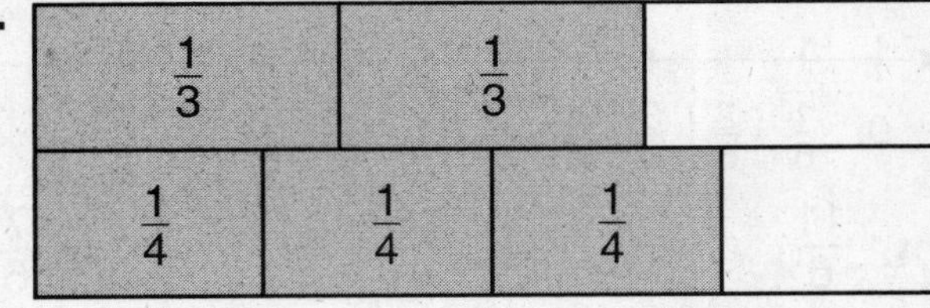

$\frac{2}{3}$ ◯ $\frac{3}{4}$

Compare. Write < or > for each ◯. Use fraction strips or a number line if needed.

5. $\frac{1}{3}$ ◯ $\frac{1}{6}$

6. $\frac{3}{4}$ ◯ $\frac{4}{4}$

7. $\frac{5}{6}$ ◯ $\frac{3}{6}$

8. $\frac{6}{10}$ ◯ $\frac{9}{10}$

9. $\frac{7}{8}$ ◯ $\frac{1}{8}$

10. $\frac{1}{8}$ ◯ $\frac{1}{3}$

11. $\frac{1}{10}$ ◯ $\frac{2}{6}$

12. $\frac{1}{4}$ ◯ $\frac{1}{8}$

13. $\frac{1}{6}$ ◯ $\frac{1}{3}$

Test Prep

14. What fraction does the picture show?

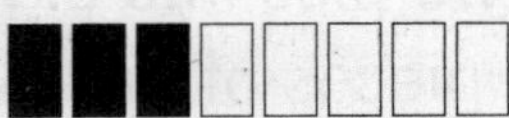

A $\frac{3}{6}$

B $\frac{2}{8}$

C $\frac{3}{8}$

D $\frac{1}{3}$

15. Joey ate $\frac{1}{8}$ of his pizza. Carl ate $\frac{1}{6}$ of his pizza. Each pizza is the same size. Who ate more pizza?

____

Use with text pages 520–521.

Name ____________________ Date ____________

Practice 19.2

Order Fractions

Order the fractions from least to greatest.

1. $\frac{1}{3}$, $\frac{1}{4}$, $\frac{1}{5}$

$\frac{1}{3}$		

$\frac{1}{4}$			

$\frac{1}{5}$				

____

2. $\frac{3}{6}$, $\frac{5}{6}$, $\frac{1}{6}$

$\frac{1}{6}$	$\frac{1}{6}$	$\frac{1}{6}$			

$\frac{1}{6}$	$\frac{1}{6}$	$\frac{1}{6}$	$\frac{1}{6}$	$\frac{1}{6}$	

$\frac{1}{6}$					

____

Order the fractions from greatest to least.

3. $\frac{2}{5}$, $\frac{4}{5}$, $\frac{1}{5}$

$\frac{1}{5}$	$\frac{1}{5}$			

$\frac{1}{5}$	$\frac{1}{5}$	$\frac{1}{5}$	$\frac{1}{5}$	

$\frac{1}{5}$				

____

4. $\frac{2}{3}$, $\frac{7}{8}$, $\frac{2}{6}$

$\frac{1}{3}$	$\frac{1}{3}$	

$\frac{1}{8}$	$\frac{1}{8}$	$\frac{1}{8}$	$\frac{1}{8}$	$\frac{1}{8}$	$\frac{1}{8}$	$\frac{1}{8}$	

$\frac{1}{6}$	$\frac{1}{6}$				

____

Order the fractions from least to greatest. Use fraction strips or draw a number line.

5. $\frac{1}{4}$ $\frac{1}{2}$ $\frac{1}{5}$ ______________

6. $\frac{3}{9}$ $\frac{5}{10}$ $\frac{2}{3}$ ______________

7. $\frac{2}{8}$ $\frac{6}{8}$ $\frac{4}{8}$ ______________

8. $\frac{6}{10}$ $\frac{3}{10}$ $\frac{8}{10}$ ______________

9. $\frac{1}{10}$ $\frac{1}{5}$ $\frac{1}{3}$ ______________

10. $\frac{3}{12}$ $\frac{1}{12}$ $\frac{8}{12}$ ______________

Test Prep

11. Which set of fractions is in order from greatest to least?

A $\frac{1}{2}, \frac{1}{5}, \frac{1}{10}$

B $\frac{0}{4}, \frac{1}{4}, \frac{3}{4}$

C $\frac{3}{5}, \frac{4}{5}, \frac{1}{5}$

D $\frac{1}{7}, \frac{1}{5}, \frac{1}{2}$

12. Kim is baking cookies. Her recipe called for $\frac{1}{2}$ cup of flour, $\frac{1}{4}$ cup water and $\frac{3}{4}$ cup of sugar. Order the fractions from least to greatest. Draw pictures to show your work.

____

Use with text pages 522–523.

Name ______________________ Date ____________

Practice 19.3

Problem-Solving Strategy: Act It Out

Use models to solve each problem.

Show your work.

1. Rachel ran $\frac{8}{10}$ mile. Karry ran $\frac{3}{4}$ mile. Who ran the greater distance?

 ____

2. There are two kinds of drums in a school band. Three-tenths of the musicians in the band play the snare drums. One-fifth of the musicians in the band play the bass drums. Which type of drum do more musicians play?

 ____

3. Emma, Abby, and Denise each bought the same size popcorn at the movies. Emma ate $\frac{3}{4}$ of her bag. Abby ate $\frac{5}{6}$ of her bag. Denise ate $\frac{2}{3}$ of her bag. Who ate the most popcorn?

 ____

4. Will $\frac{3}{5}$ and $\frac{1}{4}$ make more or less than a whole?

 ____

Use with text pages 524–526.

Name ______________________ Date ____________

Practice 19.4

Add Fractions

Add.

1.

$\frac{1}{5}$	$\frac{1}{5}$	$\frac{1}{5}$	$\frac{1}{5}$	

$\frac{2}{5} + \frac{2}{5} =$ ______

2.

$\frac{3}{6} + \frac{2}{6} =$ ______

Add. Use fraction strips or draw a picture to help you.

3. $\frac{1}{3} + \frac{1}{3} =$ ______

4. $\frac{2}{4} + \frac{1}{4} =$ ______

5. $\frac{2}{8} + \frac{3}{8} =$ ______

6. $\frac{2}{4} + \frac{1}{4} =$ ______

7. $\frac{1}{5} + \frac{3}{5} =$ ______

8. $\frac{4}{6} + \frac{1}{6} =$ ______

9. $\frac{3}{9} + \frac{4}{9} =$ ______

10. $\frac{2}{10} + \frac{3}{10} =$ ______

11. $\frac{2}{5} + \frac{1}{5} =$ ______

Algebra • Variables Find the value of *n*.

12. $\frac{n}{8} + \frac{6}{8} = \frac{7}{8}$ ______

13. $\frac{3}{5} + \frac{n}{5} = \frac{4}{5}$ ______

14. $\frac{4}{7} + \frac{n}{7} = \frac{5}{7}$ ______

15. $\frac{n}{9} + \frac{2}{9} = \frac{7}{9}$ ______

16. $\frac{3}{7} + \frac{n}{7} = \frac{6}{7}$ ______

17. $\frac{1}{4} + \frac{n}{4} = \frac{2}{4}$ ______

Test Prep

18. Find the sum of $\frac{1}{9}$ and $\frac{3}{9}$.

A $\frac{2}{9}$ **C** $\frac{4}{9}$

B $\frac{5}{9}$ **D** $\frac{6}{9}$

19. What is the sum of $\frac{6}{10}$ and $\frac{2}{10}$? Draw a picture to help you solve the problem.

____

Name ______________________ Date ____________

Subtract Fractions

Subtract.

1.

$\frac{3}{6} - \frac{1}{6} =$ ______

2.

$\frac{4}{5} - \frac{2}{5} =$ ______

Subtract. Use fraction strips or draw a picture to help you.

3. $\frac{6}{8} - \frac{1}{8}$ ______

4. $\frac{5}{7} - \frac{3}{7}$ ______

5. $\frac{4}{9} - \frac{1}{9}$ ______

6. $\frac{2}{6} - \frac{1}{6}$ ______

7. $\frac{7}{8} - \frac{2}{8}$ ______

8. $\frac{9}{9} - \frac{7}{9}$ ______

9. $\frac{3}{5} - \frac{1}{5}$ ______

10. $\frac{4}{6} - \frac{2}{6}$ ______

11. $\frac{6}{10} - \frac{2}{10}$ ______

12. $\frac{5}{9} - \frac{1}{9}$ ______

13. $\frac{4}{5} - \frac{1}{5}$ ______

14. $\frac{2}{3} - \frac{1}{3}$ ______

Algebra • Variables Find the value of *n*.

15. $\frac{n}{10} - \frac{4}{10} = \frac{4}{10}$ ______

16. $\frac{6}{8} - \frac{n}{8} = \frac{5}{8}$ ______

17. $\frac{n}{6} - \frac{5}{6} = \frac{1}{6}$ ______

Test Prep

18. Find $\frac{9}{10} - \frac{6}{10}$.

A $\frac{15}{10}$

B $\frac{2}{10}$

C $\frac{3}{10}$

D $\frac{0}{10}$

19. Find $\frac{8}{9} - \frac{6}{9}$. Draw a picture to help you solve the problem.

____

Use with text pages 532–534.

Name ______________________ Date ____________

Tenths

Write a fraction and a decimal for each shaded part.

1.

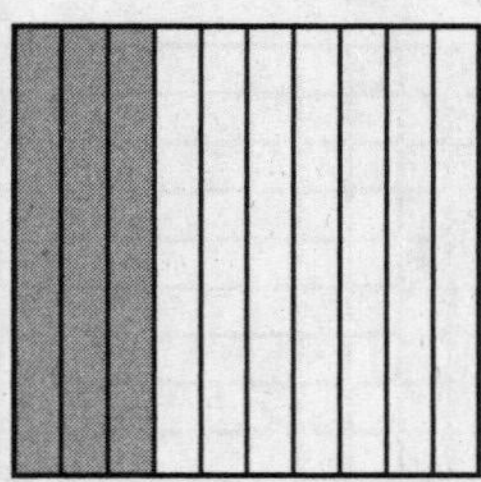

____

2.

____

3.

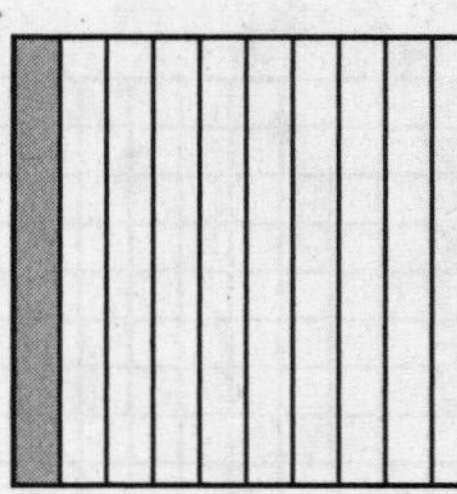

____

4.

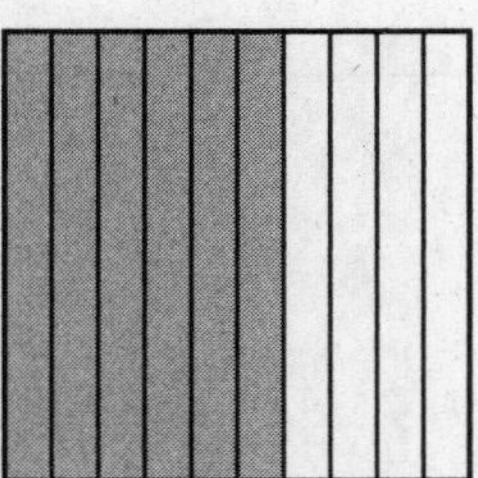

____

5.

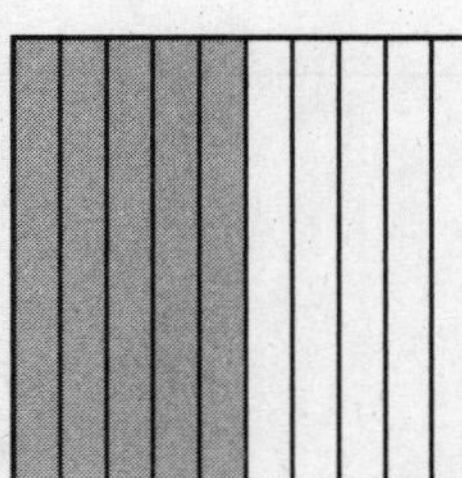

____

6.

____

Write each as a decimal.

7. $\frac{2}{10}$ ______________

8. $\frac{5}{10}$ ______________

9. three tenths ______________

10. six tenths ______________

Write each as a fraction.

11. 0.8 ______________

12. 0.4 ______________

13. one tenth ______________

14. seven tenths ______________

Test Prep

15. Which does NOT show nine tenths?

A $\frac{9}{10}$

B

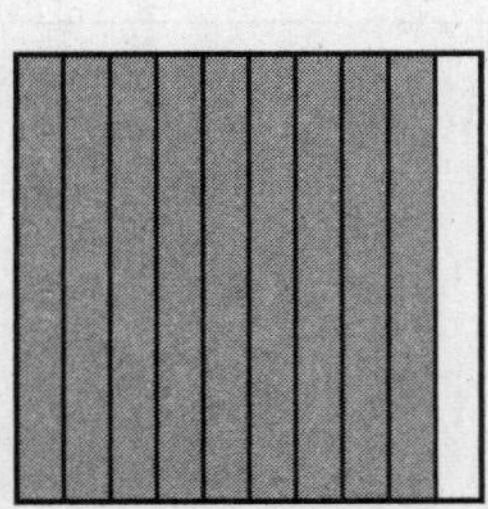

C 0.9

D $\frac{10}{9}$

16. How are $\frac{4}{10}$ and 0.4 alike? How are they different?

____

Use with text pages 540–541.

Name ______________________ Date ______________

Practice 20.2

Hundredths

Write a fraction and a decimal for the shaded part.

1. 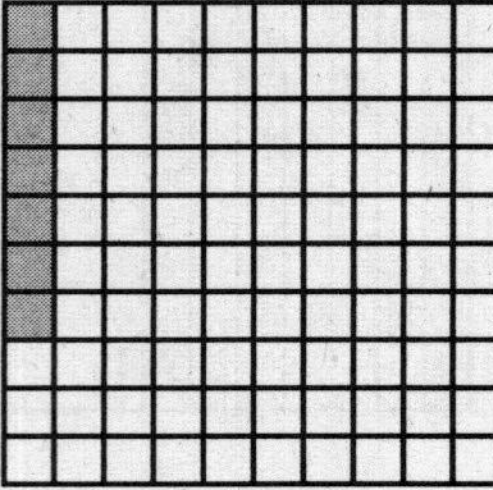

____

2. 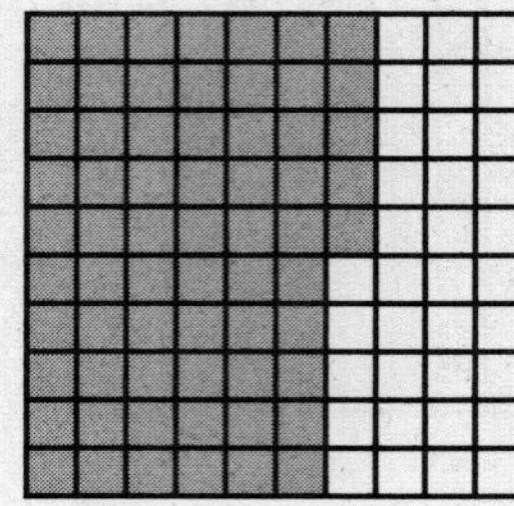

____

3. 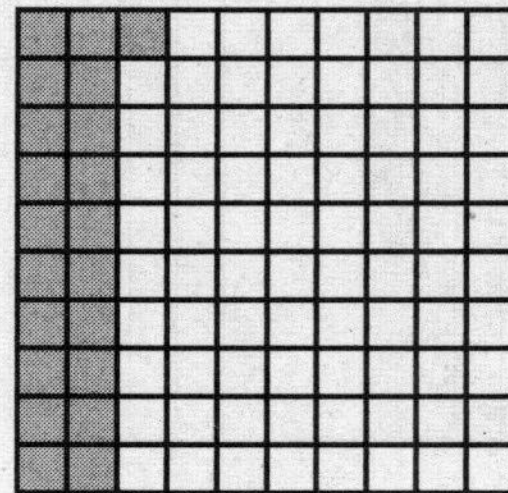

____

Write each as a decimal.

4. $\frac{30}{100}$ ______________

5. $\frac{6}{100}$ ______________

6. $\frac{57}{100}$ ______________

7. seventeen hundredths ______________

Write each as a fraction.

8. 0.12 ______________

9. 0.08 ______________

10. 0.72 ______________

11. ninety hundredths ______________

Test Prep

12. Which decimal shows $\frac{5}{100}$?

A 05.0 **C** 0.5

B 0.05 **D** 5.0

13. Why is there a 0 after the decimal point in 0.06?

____

____

Use with text pages 542–543.

Name ______________________ Date ____________

Practice 20.3

Decimals Greater Than 1

Write a mixed number and a decimal for the shaded part.

1. 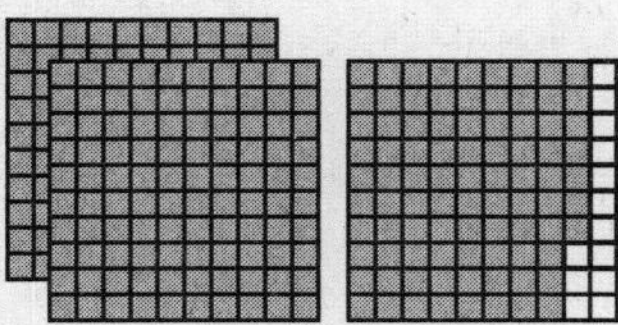

____

2. 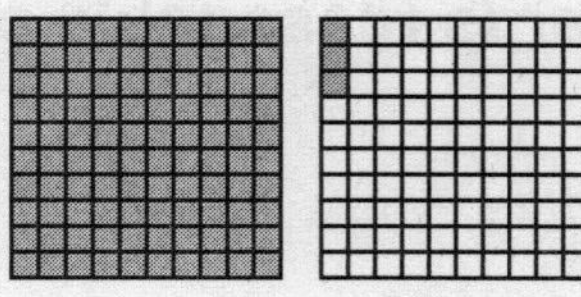

____

3. 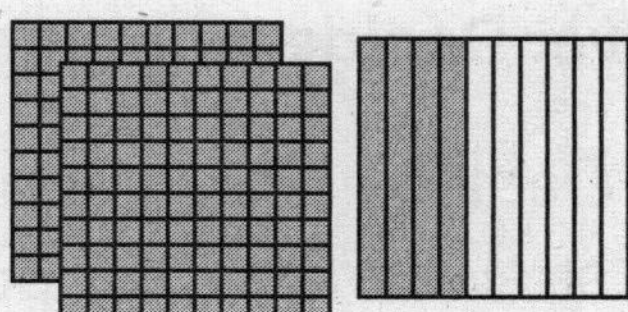

____

4. 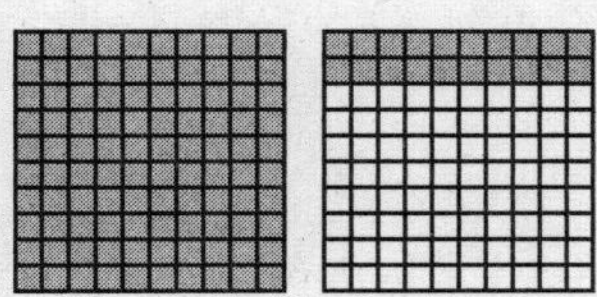

____

5. 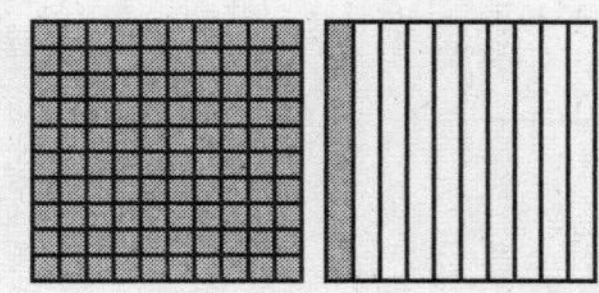

____

6. 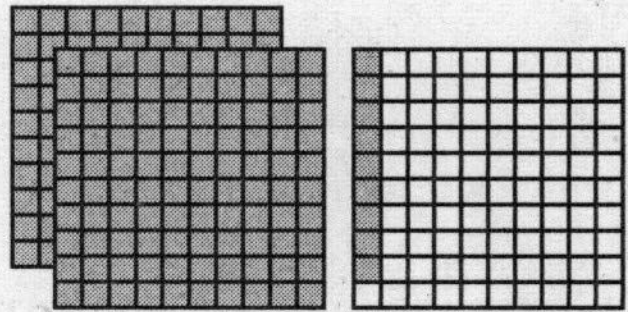

____

Write each as a decimal.

7. $3\frac{4}{100}$ ______

8. $4\frac{22}{100}$ ______

9. $6\frac{9}{10}$ ______

10. $1\frac{72}{100}$ ______

11. $8\frac{74}{100}$ ______

12. five and four tenths ______

13. nine and forty-nine hundredths ______

14. two and one hundredth ______

15. Choose the mixed number that is the same as 4.03.

A $3\frac{4}{100}$

B $4\frac{3}{100}$

C $4\frac{3}{10}$

D $4\frac{30}{100}$

16. Which decimal is greater than one: 0.83 or 1.83? Explain how you know.

____

____

____

Use with text pages 544–545.

Name ______________________ Date ____________

Practice 20.4

Problem-Solving Decision: Reasonable Answers

Solve. Decide whether the answer is reasonable or not.

Show your work.

1. Danielle bought a package of strawberries. She put $\frac{1}{8}$ of the strawberries in each of 3 fruit salads. Danielle says that she has $\frac{3}{8}$ of the strawberries left. Is this reasonable?

   ____

2. Sam needs to do yard work for 1 hour to get his allowance. He mowed the lawn for $\frac{3}{4}$ hour and weeded the garden for $\frac{1}{4}$ hour. Sam thinks that he has to do another $\frac{1}{4}$ hour of yard work to get his allowance. Is this reasonable?

   ____

3. Jack painted $\frac{1}{3}$ of the doghouse in the morning and $\frac{1}{3}$ in the afternoon. He says that $\frac{1}{3}$ of the doghouse is not painted. Is this reasonable?

   ____

4. Adela used $\frac{3}{10}$ of a container of frozen yogurt to make a sundae. Trevor used $\frac{4}{10}$ of the yogurt. Manuel says that only $\frac{1}{10}$ of the yogurt is left. Is this reasonable?

   ____

Use with text page 546.

Name ______________________ Date ____________

Practice 20.5

Compare and Order Decimals

Compare. Write >, <, or = in each ◯.

1. 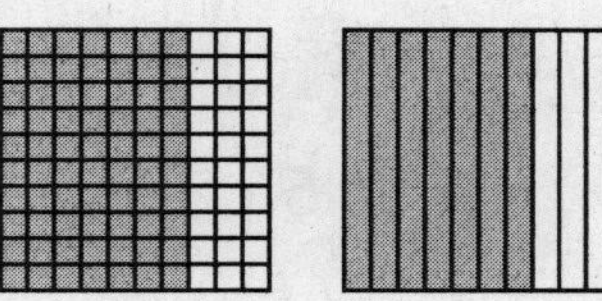

0.70 ◯ 0.7

2. 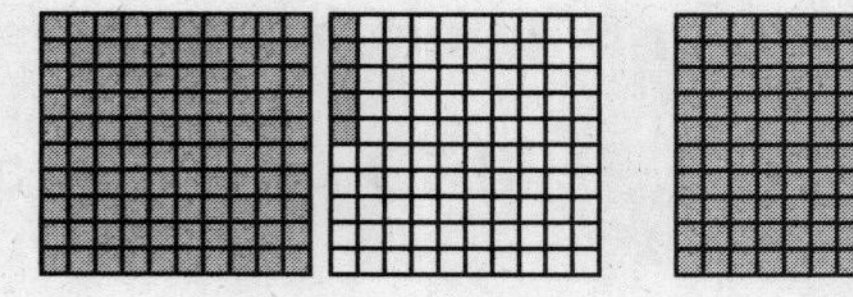

1.05 ◯ 1.5

3. 3.8 ◯ 3.6

4. 0.71 ◯ 0.61

5. 3.3 ◯ 3.30

6. 0.83 ◯ 0.87

7. 6.05 ◯ 6.5

8. 7.26 ◯ 7.24

Order the decimals from least to greatest.

9. 0.57 0.87 0.78

______ ______ ______

10. 7.8 6.4 7.9

______ ______ ______

11. 9.12 9.14 8.12

______ ______ ______

12. 2.35 0.52 0.62

______ ______ ______

13. 6.04 6.03 6.05

______ ______ ______

14. 1.44 0.44 1.43

______ ______ ______

Test Prep

15. Which decimal is greater than 0.8?

A 0.86 **C** 0.68

B 0.80 **D** 0.78

16. Which decimal is greater, 2.34 or 2.31? Explain how you know.

____

Name ____________________ Date ____________

Practice 20.6

Compare and Order Fractions and Decimals

Compare. Write >, <, or = in each ◯.

1. $\frac{4}{10}$ ◯ $\frac{2}{10}$
2. 0.03 ◯ $\frac{3}{100}$
3. $\frac{6}{10}$ ◯ 0.06
4. 0.5 ◯ $\frac{7}{10}$
5. $\frac{1}{10}$ ◯ 0.01
6. 0.08 ◯ $\frac{9}{100}$
7. $\frac{9}{10}$ ◯ 0.9
8. 0.06 ◯ $\frac{5}{100}$
9. 0.43 ◯ $\frac{40}{100}$
10. 0.2 ◯ $\frac{2}{100}$
11. 0.66 ◯ $\frac{68}{100}$
12. 0.04 ◯ $\frac{3}{100}$
13. 0.42 ◯ $\frac{3}{100}$
14. $\frac{5}{100}$ ◯ 0.11
15. $\frac{35}{100}$ ◯ 0.35
16. 0.89 ◯ $\frac{90}{100}$

Order the numbers from least to greatest.

17. 0.04 0.05 $\frac{2}{100}$ ____________
18. $\frac{3}{10}$ 0.1 $\frac{6}{10}$ ____________
19. 0.15 $\frac{18}{100}$ 0.12 ____________
20. 0.36 $\frac{41}{100}$ $\frac{39}{100}$ ____________
21. $\frac{61}{100}$ 0.60 0.57 ____________
22. 0.15 $\frac{25}{100}$ 0.17 ____________

Test Prep

23. Choose the decimal that is less than $\frac{56}{100}$.

    A 0.56
    B 0.65
    C 0.53
    D 0.58

24. Which number is greater, 0.73 or $\frac{64}{100}$? Explain how you know.

    ____

Use with text pages 550–551.

Name ______________________ Date ____________

Practice 20.7

Relate Decimals, Fractions, and Money

Complete the table below. Use play money to help you.

	Coins	Number of Cents	Fraction of a Dollar	Values as a Decimal
1.	7 pennies			
2.	6 dimes			
3.	3 quarters			
4.	37 pennies			
5.	1 nickel			
6.	1 half-dollar			

Write each amount as a fraction of a dollar.

7. $0.35 = __________ of a dollar

8. $0.81 = __________ of a dollar

9. $0.09 = __________ of a dollar

10. $0.70 = __________ of a dollar

11. $0.10 = __________ of a dollar

12. $0.97 = __________ of a dollar

13. $0.30 = __________ of a dollar

14. $0.05 = __________ of a dollar

Test Prep

15. Choose the amount that matches the group of coins.

A $0.07

B $0.77

C $0.70

D $7.00

16. Shade the hundredths model to show the part of $1.00 that is $0.45.

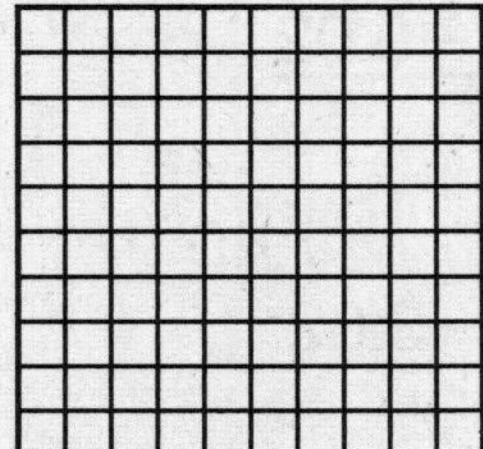

Name ______________________ Date ____________

Practice 20.8

Add and Subtract Decimals

Add or subtract.

1. 3.6 + 2.1

2. 5.4 + 3.8

3. 0.83 + 2.81

4. 4.77 + 8.54

5. 1.29 + 3.94

6. 7.8 − 6.3

7. 6.1 − 3.2

8. 7.84 − 3.91

9. 6.97 − 5.88

10. 8.55 − 2.09

11. 5.3 + 2.7 ______

12. 7.49 + 1.55 ______

13. 3.22 − 1.61 ______

14. 5.0 − 0.5 ______

Complete each table. If the rule is not given, write the rule.

	Rule: Add 2.2	
	Input	**Output**
15.	1.0	
16.	1.5	
17.		4.2
18.	2.5	

	Rule: Subtract 0.7	
	Input	**Output**
19.	4.0	
20.	3.0	
21.		1.2
22.	0.9	

23.

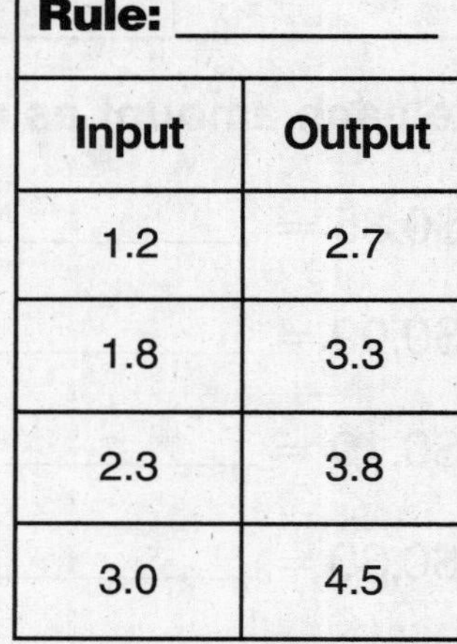

Rule: ______	
Input	**Output**
1.2	2.7
1.8	3.3
2.3	3.8
3.0	4.5

Test Prep

24. Choose the correct way to write 7.40 − 3.02.

A 7.40 − 3.02 (misaligned)

B 7.40 − 3.02 (misaligned)

C 7.40 − 3.02

D 7.40 − 3.02 (misaligned)

25. Explain how to add 6.18 + 2.71.

____

Use with text pages 556–558.

Name ______________________ Date ____________

Practice 20.9

Problem-Solving Application: Use Money

Solve. **Show your work.**

1. Paco bought a package of stickers for $2.25 and a glitter pen for $2.19. He gave the clerk 1 five-dollar bill. How much change will he get?

   ____

2. Scrapbooks cost $2. How many scrapbooks could you buy with 2 five-dollar bills and 8 quarters?

   ____

3. Linda paid $21.50 for three stuffed animals. The teddy bear cost $7.25. The giraffe cost $6.15. How much did the elephant cost?

   ____

4. Elmore has 1 ten-dollar bill, 3 five-dollar bills, and 2 one-dollar bills in his bank. How much more money does he need to buy a train set that costs $31.95?

   ____

5. Tina bought three autograph books for $4 each. Autograph books went on sale a week later for $3.50 each. How much could Tina have saved by buying the autograph books when they were on sale?

   ____

Name ______________________ Date ____________

Practice 21.1

Multiply Multiples of 10, 100, and 1,000

Use a basic fact and patterns to help you find each product.

1. 4 × 3 = ______
   4 × 30 = ______
   4 × 300 = ______
   4 × 3,000 = ______

2. 5 × 2 = ______
   5 × 20 = ______
   5 × 200 = ______
   5 × 2,000 = ______

3. 7 × 4 = ______
   7 × 40 = ______
   7 × 400 = ______
   7 × 4,000 = ______

4. 2 × 2 = ______
   2 × 20 = ______
   2 × 200 = ______
   2 × 2,000 = ______

5. 5 × 5 = ______
   5 × 50 = ______
   5 × 500 = ______
   5 × 5,000 = ______

6. 9 × 4 = ______
   9 × 40 = ______
   9 × 400 = ______
   9 × 4,000 = ______

Find each product.

7. 7 × 20 ______
8. 2 × 60 ______
9. 3 × 50 ______
10. 5 × 80 ______
11. 9 × 400 ______
12. 3 × 700 ______
13. 7 × 400 ______
14. 3 × 500 ______
15. 2 × 9,000 ______
16. 9 × 6,000 ______
17. 8 × 9,000 ______
18. 6 × 4,000 ______

Test Prep

19. What is the product of 9 × 400?

    A 36 **C** 360
    B 36,000 **D** 3,600

20. A trip from New Orleans to Houston and back is about 700 miles. How many miles a month would you travel if you made this trip twice a month?

    ____

Use with text pages 580–581.

Name ______________________ Date ______________

Practice 21.2

Model Multiplication

Use base-ten blocks to help you find each product.

1. 4×12 ______
2. 3×22 ______
3. 4×18 ______
4. 6×13 ______
5. 3×33 ______
6. 5×15 ______
7. 4×23 ______
8. 4×12 ______
9. 5×17 ______
10. 4×15 ______
11. 5×12 ______
12. 5×21 ______
13. 3×17 ______
14. 2×28 ______
15. 5×18 ______
16. 6×15 ______

Tell what multiplication sentence is shown by the blocks.

17. 

____

18. 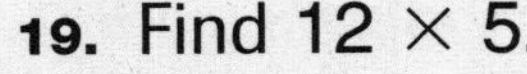

____

Test Prep

19. Find 12×5.

A 50 C 65

B 60 D 61

20. How much greater is the product of 3 and 26 than the product of 2 and 26?

____

Use with text pages 582–583.

Name ______________________ Date ____________

Practice 21.3

Estimate Products

Estimate each product.

1. 58×6 **2.** 24×4 **3.** 41×3 **4.** 945×7 **5.** 462×8

6. 63×2 **7.** 26×7 **8.** 62×3 **9.** 532×4 **10.** 354×3

11. 47×5 ______ **12.** 56×6 ______ **13.** 324×3 ______ **14.** 699×8 ______

15. 32×6 ______ **16.** 719×2 ______ **17.** 589×8 ______ **18.** 425×8 ______

Algebra • Symbols Compare. Write >, < or = for each ◯.

19. 61×5 ◯ 38×3 **20.** 30×3 ◯ 9×12 **21.** 4×40 ◯ 80×2

22. 153×4 ◯ 163×4 **23.** 3×20 ◯ 20×3 **24.** 60×6 ◯ 5×60

Test Prep

25. Which is the best estimate of 294×5?

A 1,600 **C** 150

B 15,000 **D** 1,500

26. Estimate to decide if 28×6 is greater than or less than 28×5. Explain your answer.

____

____

____

Use with text pages 584–586.

Name ______________________ Date ______________

Practice 21.4

Multiply 2-Digit Numbers by 1-Digit Numbers

Find each product.

1. 17×4

2. 67×3

3. 22×8

4. 42×5

5. 39×3

6. 56×3

7. 23×2

8. 37×4

9. 4×14 ______

10. 3×18 ______

11. 5×22 ______

12. 6×31 ______

13. 7×42 ______

14. 6×14 ______

Algebra • Functions Complete each table.

	Rule: Multiply by 5	
	Input	**Output**
	25	125
15.	14	
16.	11	
17.		50

	Rule: Multiply by 4	
	Input	**Output**
18.		44
	32	128
19.	65	
20.	80	

21.	**Rule:**	
	Input	**Output**
	34	204
	22	132
22.	16	
23.	12	

Test Prep

24. Find the product of 4 and 23.

A 90 **C** 92

B 98 **D** 94

25. At Hill High School's music festival 8 chorus groups compete for the national singing title. Each group has 24 students. How many students compete in all?

____

Name ______________________ Date ______________

Practice 21.5

Multiply 3-Digit Numbers by 1-Digit Numbers

Find each product.

1. $\begin{array}{r} 214 \\ \times \ 2 \\ \hline \end{array}$

2. $\begin{array}{r} 151 \\ \times \ 4 \\ \hline \end{array}$

3. $\begin{array}{r} 419 \\ \times \ 2 \\ \hline \end{array}$

4. $\begin{array}{r} 219 \\ \times \ 4 \\ \hline \end{array}$

5. $\begin{array}{r} 217 \\ \times \ 3 \\ \hline \end{array}$

6. $\begin{array}{r} 232 \\ \times \ 4 \\ \hline \end{array}$

7. $\begin{array}{r} 132 \\ \times \ 3 \\ \hline \end{array}$

8. $\begin{array}{r} 354 \\ \times \ 2 \\ \hline \end{array}$

9. $\begin{array}{r} 124 \\ \times \ 4 \\ \hline \end{array}$

10. $\begin{array}{r} 141 \\ \times \ 5 \\ \hline \end{array}$

11. 3×162 ______

12. 2×448 ______

13. 5×118 ______

14. 3×316 ______

15. 2×234 ______

16. 3×131 ______

17. 2×317 ______

18. 2×428 ______

Algebra • Symbols Compare. Write >, < or = for each ◯.

19. 410×6 ◯ 400×6

20. 73×2 ◯ $100 + 30 + 6$

21. 312×3 ◯ 312×3

22. 3×171 ◯ $(3 \times 100) + (7 \times 1)$

23. 102×2 ◯ 201×2

24. 40×40 ◯ 80×20

25. Find the missing factor.
$4 \times$ ______ $= 800$.

A 100 **C** 120

B 200 **D** 300

26. Find the product.
312×2

____

Use with text pages 592–593.

Name ____________________ Date ____________

Practice 21.6

Problem-Solving Strategy: Solve a Simpler Problem

Use easier numbers to help you solve each problem.

Show your work.

1. A baseball park holds 3,000 people. One night there were 1,257 empty seats. On another night, there were 985 empty seats. How many seats were occupied the two nights? ____________

2. There are 225 beads in a package of colored beads. April buys 3 packages and Rachel buys 4 packages. How many beads will the girls have altogether? ____________

3. The distance around a track is 440 yards. Katie runs around the track 3 times and Karen runs around the track 5 times. How many yards will the two girls run in all? ____________

4. A horse drawn carriage ride takes tourists on a 6 mile tour of a city. There were 165 tours in June, 180 tours in July, and 142 tours in August. How many miles did the carriage travel during those three months? ____________

5. It takes 334 sheets of paper to print a report. Mr. Arnold needs 3 copies of the report for his job. Mrs. Gomez needs 4 copies of the report for her job. How many sheets of paper will be used to print the reports in all? ____________

Use with text pages 594–596.

Name ______________________ Date ____________

Practice 21.7

Regrouping Twice

Multiply. Regroup if needed.

1. $\begin{array}{r} 105 \\ \times \quad 8 \\ \hline \end{array}$

2. $\begin{array}{r} 198 \\ \times \quad 4 \\ \hline \end{array}$

3. $\begin{array}{r} 619 \\ \times \quad 3 \\ \hline \end{array}$

4. $\begin{array}{r} 728 \\ \times \quad 2 \\ \hline \end{array}$

5. $\begin{array}{r} 1{,}191 \\ \times \quad 6 \\ \hline \end{array}$

6. $\begin{array}{r} 2{,}268 \\ \times \quad 3 \\ \hline \end{array}$

7. $\begin{array}{r} 4{,}321 \\ \times \quad 6 \\ \hline \end{array}$

8. $\begin{array}{r} 3{,}546 \\ \times \quad 2 \\ \hline \end{array}$

9. 7 × 115 ______

10. 5 × 313 ______

11. 4 × 521 ______

12. 2 × 579

13. 5 × 1,316 ______

14. 6 × 1,141 ______

15. 4 × 6,511

16. 5 × 3,310

Compare the products. Write >, <, or = for each ◯.

17. 275 × 4 ◯ 4 × 275

18. 3 × 138 ◯ 2 × 156

19. 4 × 174 ◯ 5 × 129

20. 2 × 8,528 ◯ 3 × 5,412

Find the missing digit. Show your work.

21. $\begin{array}{r} 374 \\ \times \quad 3 \\ \hline 1{,}12\blacksquare \end{array}$

22. $\begin{array}{r} 418 \\ \times \quad 6 \\ \hline 2{,}5\blacksquare 8 \end{array}$

23. $\begin{array}{r} 571 \\ \times \quad 2 \\ \hline 1{,}\blacksquare 42 \end{array}$

24. $\begin{array}{r} 5{,}018 \\ \times \quad 4 \\ \hline 2\blacksquare{,}072 \end{array}$

Test Prep

25. Jane's calculator shows 1,053. Which of these products did she multiply?

A 5 × 333 **C** 3 × 341

B 5 × 355 **D** 3 × 351

26. Find the product 4 × 1,352.

____

Use with text pages 598–600.

Name ______________________ Date ____________

Practice 21.8

Multiply Money

Estimate, then multiply.

1. $1.25 × 5
2. $3.24 × 6
3. $1.75 × 3
4. $4.49 × 2
5. $5.79 × 3

6. $1.99 × 3
7. $4.26 × 5
8. $2.72 × 2
9. $3.15 × 5
10. $3.10 × 8

11. 6 × $5.41 ______
12. 4 × $2.29 ______
13. 9 × $1.19 ______
14. 2 × $1.36 ______

15. 5 × $6.19 ______
16. 3 × $2.30 ______
17. 6 × $2.89 ______
18. 4 × $1.95 ______

Algebra • Functions Complete each table.

	Rule: Multiply by 3	
	Input	**Output**
	$2.32	$6.96
19.	$3.63	
20.	$1.25	
21.		$7.50

	Rule: Multiply by 4	
	Input	**Output**
22.	$2.13	
23.	$4.26	
24.		$12.96
25.	$1.39	

26.	Rule:	
	Input	**Output**
	$3.25	$6.50
	$5.50	$11.00
27.	$7.58	
28.	$9.18	

Test Prep

29. Find the product.
4 × $2.29

A $9.16 **C** $8.16

B $9.17 **D** $9.26

30. If you bought 6 cans of vegetables for $0.65 each, would you spend more than $5.00? Explain your answer.

____

Use with text pages 602–604.

Name ______________________ Date ______________

Practice 22.1

Use Mental Math to Divide

Use a basic fact and patterns to find each quotient.

1. 6 ÷ 3 ______

60 ÷ 3 ______

600 ÷ 3 ______

2. 45 ÷ 5 ______

450 ÷ 5 ______

4,500 ÷ 5 ______

3. 15 ÷ 3 ______

150 ÷ 3 ______

1,500 ÷ 3 ______

4. 18 ÷ 9 ______

180 ÷ 9 ______

1,800 ÷ 9 ______

5. 63 ÷ 9 ______

630 ÷ 9 ______

6,300 ÷ 9 ______

6. 40 ÷ 8 ______

400 ÷ 8 ______

4,000 ÷ 8 ______

Divide.

7. 480 ÷ 6 ______

8. 2,700 ÷ 3 ______

9. 400 ÷ 4 ______

10. 800 ÷ 2 ______

11. 3,600 ÷ 6 ______

12. 1,800 ÷ 2 ______

13. 900 ÷ 3 ______

14. 100 ÷ 5 ______

15. 8,100 ÷ 9 ______

16. 3,000 ÷ 6 ______

17. 1,400 ÷ 2 ______

18. 1,200 ÷ 4 ______

Test Prep

19. Which number sentence is correct?

A 240 ÷ 4 = 70

B 280 ÷ 4 = 70

C 250 ÷ 5 = 55

D 200 ÷ 5 = 45

20. How can you use 16 ÷ 8 to find 1,600 ÷ 8?

____

Use with text pages 610–611.

Name ______________________ Date ____________

Practice 22.2

Model Division with Remainders

Use the picture to divide.

1. 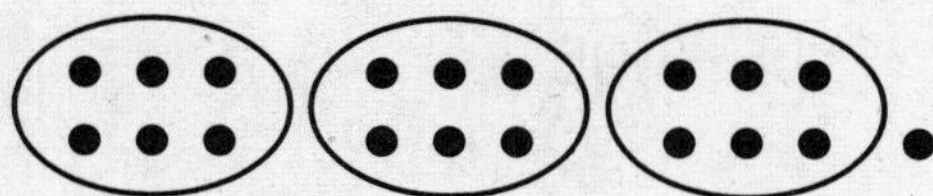

____

2. 

____

3. 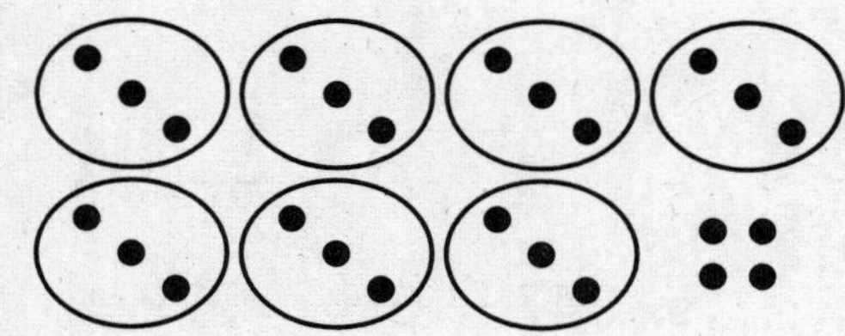

____

4. 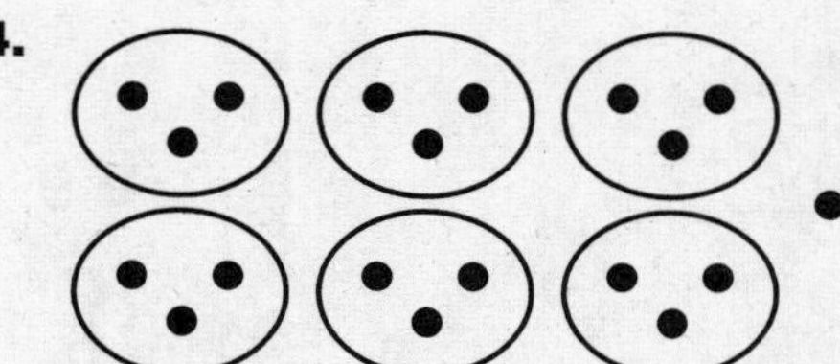

____

Divide. Use counters and repeated subtraction to help you.

5. 16 ÷ 4 ______

6. 23 ÷ 3 ______

7. 33 ÷ 6 ______

8. 42 ÷ 6 ______

9. 19 ÷ 3 ______

10. 81 ÷ 9 ______

11. 39 ÷ 8 ______

12. 72 ÷ 9 ______

Divide. Use counters or draw a picture to help you.

13. Divide 12 into 5 equal groups.

____

14. Divide 25 into 6 equal groups.

____

Test Prep

15. What is the correct answer to 36 ÷ 7?

A 5 R1 **C** 6

B 7 R1 **D** 8

16. Pat says 15 ÷ 4 is 3 R3. Phil says it is 2 R7. Who is right?

____

Use with text pages 612–614.

Name ______________________ Date ______________

Practice 22.3

Estimate Quotients

Estimate. Write the compatible numbers you used.

1. $8\overline{)63}$ ______

2. $4\overline{)83}$ ______

3. $5\overline{)95}$ ______

4. $4\overline{)331}$ ______

5. $4\overline{)194}$ ______

6. $8\overline{)638}$ ______

7. 237 ÷ 6 ______

8. 541 ÷ 6 ______

9. 347 ÷ 5 ______

Estimate to decide if each quotient is greater than 50 or less than 50. Use this division example to help you: 250 ÷ 5 = 50.

10. 235 ÷ 5 ______

11. 341 ÷ 3 ______

12. 283 ÷ 9 ______

13. 333 ÷ 4 ______

Algebra • Expressions Compare. Use > or < for each ◯.

14. 17 ÷ 5 ◯ 18 ÷ 2

15. 23 ÷ 4 ◯ 22 ÷ 7

16. 14 ÷ 7 ◯ 16 ÷ 2

Test Prep

17. What basic fact could you use to help find 15 ÷ 2?

A 5 × 2 = 10
B 6 × 2 = 12
C 7 × 2 = 14
D 9 × 2 = 18

18. Mark estimated 165 ÷ 5 as 30. Is his estimate greater than or less than the actual answer?

____

Use with text pages 616–618.

Name ______________________ Date ____________

Practice 22.4

Two-Digit Quotients

Use base-ten blocks to help you divide.

1. $3\overline{)66}$ **2.** $7\overline{)74}$ **3.** $3\overline{)65}$ **4.** $4\overline{)86}$ **5.** $2\overline{)62}$

6. $3\overline{)97}$ **7.** $2\overline{)26}$ **8.** $4\overline{)47}$ **9.** $3\overline{)99}$ **10.** $2\overline{)43}$

11. 92 ÷ 3 ______ **12.** 68 ÷ 6 ______ **13.** 83 ÷ 2 ______ **14.** 69 ÷ 2 ______

Algebra • Symbols Use >, <, or = for each ◯.

15. 48 ÷ 2 ◯ 20 **16.** 48 ÷ 4 ◯ 12 **17.** 200 ÷ 5 ◯ 50

18. 13 ◯ 88 ÷ 4 **19.** 14 ◯ 22 ÷ 2 **20.** 240 ÷ 6 ◯ 40

21. 12 ◯ 63 ÷ 3 **22.** 50 ◯ 320 ÷ 8 **23.** 100 ÷ 5 ◯ 10

Test Prep

24. What is 55 divided by 5?

A 9 **C** 10

B 11 **D** 12

25. Drew wants to put 69 paper clips into 3 boxes. He wants the same number of paper clips in each box. How many paper clips should he put in each box? Explain how you found your answer.

____

____

____

Use with text pages 620–621.

Name ______________________ Date ______________

Practice 22.5

Problem-Solving Application: Interpret Remainders

Solve.

Show your work.

1. At Raymond's Peach Farm, 56 peaches are being packed in boxes. Each box holds 9 peaches. How many boxes are needed?

____

2. Ricky has to plant 73 peach trees. He can plant 8 peach trees each day. How many days will it take Ricky to plant all the peach trees?

____

3. Shelia brought 29 peaches home. She divided them equally into 3 boxes to give to her friends. How many peaches will be left over?

____

4. Raymond would like to sell 60 boxes of peaches this week. If he sells 9 boxes each day, how many days will it take him to sell all 60 boxes?

____

5. Mr. Russell has $15 to spend at the peach farm. Peaches are sold at $4 per dozen. How many dozen peaches can Mr. Russell buy?

____

Use with text pages 622–623.

Name ______________________ Date ____________

Practice 22.6

Three-Digit Quotients

Divide and check.

1. $2\overline{)238}$
2. $6\overline{)696}$
3. $4\overline{)478}$
4. $4\overline{)466}$
5. $5\overline{)560}$
6. $3\overline{)672}$
7. $3\overline{)681}$
8. $4\overline{)853}$
9. $2\overline{)628}$
10. $3\overline{)948}$
11. 422 ÷ 2 ______
12. 595 ÷ 5 ______
13. 876 ÷ 4 ______
14. 598 ÷ 5 ______
15. 654 ÷ 3 ______
16. 528 ÷ 3 ______
17. 872 ÷ 4 ______
18. 477 ÷ 2 ______

19. What is 856 divided by 4?
    - **A** 223
    - **B** 214
    - **C** 225
    - **D** 242
20. Find the quotient. Explain how you found your answer.

    957 ÷ 3 = ______

    ____

    ____

Use with text pages 624–625.

Name ______________________ Date ______________

Practice 22.7

Place the First Digit

Divide. Check your answers.

1. $5\overline{)195}$
2. $2\overline{)188}$
3. $4\overline{)348}$
4. $2\overline{)132}$
5. $3\overline{)123}$
6. $6\overline{)432}$
7. $9\overline{)378}$
8. $5\overline{)490}$
9. $8\overline{)376}$
10. $3\overline{)153}$
11. 284 ÷ 4 ______
12. 146 ÷ 2 ______
13. 105 ÷ 5 ______
14. 432 ÷ 8 ______

Algebra • Equations Solve for *n*.

15. 848 ÷ 2 = *n*
    848 ÷ 4 = *n*
    848 ÷ 8 = *n*
    ______
    ______
    ______
16. 48 ÷ 2 = *n*
    48 ÷ 4 = *n*
    48 ÷ 8 = *n*
    ______
    ______
    ______
17. 536 ÷ 2 = *n*
    536 ÷ 4 = *n*
    536 ÷ 8 = *n*
    ______
    ______
    ______
18. 864 ÷ 2 = *n*
    864 ÷ 4 = *n*
    864 ÷ 8 = *n*
    ______
    ______
    ______

Test Prep

19. Find 792 ÷ 8.

    A 89 **C** 97

    B 98 **D** 99

20. A meeting room has 150 seats. There are 5 rows. How many seats are in each row? Explain how you found your answer.

    ____

    ____

    ____

Use with text pages 626–627.

Name ______________________ Date __________

Practice 22.8

Divide Money

Divide. Model with coins and bills if you wish.

1. $3\overline{)\$3.75}$
2. $4\overline{)\$4.88}$
3. $3\overline{)\$9.78}$
4. $2\overline{)\$6.42}$

5. $5.96 ÷ 2 ______
6. $8.44 ÷ 2 ______
7. $7.14 ÷ 2 ______
8. $6.96 ÷ 6 ______

Algebra • Functions Complete each table. If the rule is not given, write the rule.

	Rule: Divide by 4	
	Input	**Output**
	$8.00	$2.00
9.	$9.00	
10.	$1.24	
11.		$3.00
12.	$4.04	

	Rule: Divide by 3	
	Input	**Output**
13.	$9.36	
14.		$2.11
15.		$1.14
16.	$1.32	
17.	$1.02	

	Rule: ______	
18.	**Input**	**Output**
	$4.22	$2.11
	$6.42	$3.21
19.	$1.20	
20.	$5.24	
21.	$8.48	

Algebra • Equations Solve for *n*.

22. $n \div 2 = \$4.00$ ______
23. $\$1.60 \div 2 = n$ ______
24. $\$2.14 = n \div 4$ ______

Test Prep

25. $6.33 ÷ 3 = ______

A $1.22 C $2.11

B $2.21 D $2.22

26. Kay bought 4 notebooks for $8.64. What was the cost of 1 notebook?

____

Use with text pages 628–630.